"AND HE AWOKE AND REBUKED
THE WIND AND SAID
TO THE SEA, 'PEACE! BE STILL!'
AND THE WIND CEASED,
AND THERE WAS A GREAT CALM."

-Matthew 4:39

ANCHOR
my soul

ANCHOR
my soul

Andrea P. Bourgeois

Arabelle Publishing, LLC
Chesterfield, VA

ANCHOR
my soul

ARABELLE PUBLISHING
PO Box 2841
Chesterfield, VA 23832
www.arabellebooks.com
IG: @ArabellePublishing
IG: @ArabelleBooks

Credits:
Cover Copyright @ 2021 by Arabelle Publishing, LLC.
Interior Design by Julie Basinski

Library of Congress Control Number: 2021940933
Subjects: Memoir, Christian Living, Christian Spiritual Growth
ISBN: 978-1-7356-3281-0 (trade paperback)

Printed in the United States of America, 2021

Group Sales:
Books are available with special quantity discounts when purchased in bulk directly from the publisher. This discount applies to corporations, organizations, and special interest groups. For more information, email the publisher at arabellepublishing@gmail.com

TO THE RESIDENTS AND BUSINESS OWNERS
OF MOSS BLUFF, LAKE CHARLES, AND ALL
SURROUNDING CITIES IN SOUTHWEST LOUISIANA
AND SOUTHEAST TEXAS DESTROYED
BY HURRICANE LAURA ON
AUGUST 27, 2020 AND THEN AGAIN BY
HURRICANE DELTA ON OCTOBER 9, 2020.

TABLE OF
CONTENTS

CHAPTER

PREFACE

Jordan Sellers, my marketing consultant, and I were brainstorming ideas and ways to reach women in their pain during the unexpected, quarantined spring and summer of 2020. I pitched the idea of doing an online summit for women to share their "pain into purpose" stories on a virtual platform. He jumped on board and we planned our first Pain into Purpose Virtual Summit in six weeks and launched that July.

Shortly after, my publisher contacted me with the idea to turn the stories shared on the summit into a memoir devotional. I contacted all thirty speakers for the opportunity to write and contribute their stories in close to 1000 words. Twenty-five speakers committed with short notice, and they began emailing me their stories.

A few days before Hurricane Laura hit my hometown, I received the book contract. Without having time to review it because of mandatory evacuations from our governor, I knew I'd need to find an Internet connection and a printer or I'd miss this opportunity.

After the storm, I drove three hours to my in-law's house to review, print, and sign the contract. Then I brainstormed the theme, and wrote the devotional. It wasn't until that first day there that the theme of overcoming storms in our life was revealed.

The Lord orchestrated the summit, birthed this book, and inspired me to write the words through the emotions caused by the actual storm my family and I were facing.

MY PRAYER IS FOR THIS BOOK TO GIVE YOU HOPE IN YOUR STORMS IN LIFE.

ACKNOWLEDGMENTS

I have to start by thanking my husband, **BRIAN**, for believing in me and supporting me throughout this entire writing journey!

Thank you to **MY PARENTS** and **IN-LAWS** for keeping their grandson busy and entertained as I wrote this devotional with gasoline-powered generators providing cool air and power for my laptop and Wi-Fi at my in-laws house. Thank you so much for supporting me in that hectic time.

JORDAN SELLERS for all the marketing and consulting work throughout this writing journey, and trusting and co-founding with me our first Pain into Purpose Virtual Summit. This book was inspired by our successful summit and the women's stories that affected viewers around the world. [painintopurpose.co]

A huge thank you to **DIANA LEGERE** and her team working with Arabelle Publishing for giving me this idea and opportunity to turn the stories into a memoir devotional. Thank you for believing in me and my platform of helping women process their pain.

A heartfelt thank you to my intern/photographer, **MORGAN WAINWRIGHT** for all her creative insight and help.

A SPECIAL THANK YOU TO ALL THE CONTRIBUTORS:
Rachael Adams, Lindsey Belt, Becky Beresford, Season Bowers, Stephanie Broersma, Ainsley Britain, Ryan Clemons, Amy Debrucque, Chelsey DeMatteis, Megan Ethridge, Marlisa Harding, Gabbi Hartzell, Lisa Jones, Samantha LaRocque, Trudy Lonesky, Carley Marcouillier, Crystal Mayo, Natalie Miller, K. Price, Michelle Rabon, Dana Rodigue, Erin Todd, Stefanee Tolbert, Jessica Turner, and Miranda Vinson.

Thank you to **ALL THE LADIES** at Table 44, my Marco gals, the Golden Girls, and all my girls back home who've walked this writing journey with me over the years.

Thank you to **MY PRAYER TEAM** who covered me in prayer throughout this writing journey since the summer of 2019: Martha, Donna, Cheryl, Mona, Debby, Robbie, Brandi, Samantha, Alicia, and Miranda.

A special **THANK YOU** to **ROBERT** and **WANDA LACROIX** for letting me stay with you in Covington, LA to write most of this devotional during the aftermath of the hurricane. And thank you for giving my mother-in-law and son a place to play, swim, and enjoy the amenities of air conditioning and cartoons while I wrote.

INTRODUCTION

I have been living in quarantine for five months, adjusting to the new normalcy of wearing masks when I leave the house, which will continue when I return to work as a teacher.

THE WORLD HAS BEEN ON HOLD
FOR MONTHS AS WE WAIT AND SEE

what this virus does and how it spreads. It seems as though the media has hyped up the virus to instill fear in our country. Conspiracy theories don't seem so far-fetched anymore, and then two storms brew in the gulf named Marco and Laura. I finished hanging two transparent shower curtains up around my teacher's desk with binder clips and yarn to keep my desk space a "safe-space" free of germs. It's been five months since school had last been in session, and we are doing last minute preparations. The students will come face to face in a hybrid setting on Monday. I checked my email one last time before leaving school on Friday. We were instructed to power off all computers and secure them to prepare for the storms in the gulf projected to come straight for us in southwest Louisiana. I chuckled to myself, thinking these storms are not coming directly for us. Come on, 2020, this year has caused enough uncertainty and anxiety and financial burdens to so many. Really, a hurricane too?

Two days later, we got an automated call that school had been canceled because of the storms. The storms' projected paths were coming in our direction. Still, I think these storms will not be as big as RITA that hit my hometown fifteen years ago in 2005. Luckily, Marco dissipated, but Laura was growing and heading straight toward us. I thought, *The weather channel has got to be hyping this thing up for exposure.* My husband and I decided to stay, and we'd be okay because by the time the storm hit, it will be only a CAT 1 or downgraded to a tropical depression. By Tuesday of that week, I got nervous. The weather channel was projecting it to be a CAT 3 in the middle of the gulf. I sat on my in-law's wicker sofa outside their patio, watching television. I said, "If it gets to a CAT 4 in the projections, I'm leaving!" My husband, thinking there was no way this storm would come in stronger than Rita, appeased me by agreeing we'd go if it got to a CAT 4. We boarded up the windows of our home and secured our outdoor belongings just in case. Rita measured a CAT 5 in the gulf but weakened and made landfall as a CAT 3. Laura's likelihood of hitting stronger than Rita was not on our radar because we always thought those storms wouldn't come but every fifty years. Boy, were we wrong!

Wednesday morning, at 5 a.m., I woke to a text message notification on my phone that it was now projecting to be a CAT 4. A mandatory evacuation for our city was already enforced the day prior, so we knew the traffic would worsen if we waited to decide any later to get out. If we were to evacuate, we needed to leave now! I packed our family of three in less than five minutes, grabbing random things while my mind raced with the what if's. My husband, our three-and-half-year-old son, our blind golden retriever, and I drove east to our extended family's home right outside Covington, LA. We didn't know what would happen or if we would come back to our home in one piece. We watched the weather channel around the clock with other evacuees from the storm, and as the storm grew with intensity, so did my nerves and anxiousness. Each of our parents had decided to ride out the storm in their homes. I kept praying for protection over them and our families throughout the night.

Hurricane Laura was the strongest hurricane to make landfall in over 150 years. The inner eyewall of the storm came directly over my home town. The destruction left behind is still indescribable. Not one home, yard, or business was unaffected. Oak and pine trees ripped up, snapped in half, or twisted lay on top of houses and roads across the storm's forty-mile radius. Powerline poles and transmission towers twisted and bent in half across southwest Louisiana and east Texas. I read a post from Entergy Louisiana, LLC that over 90,000 homes were out of power. The high winds caused damage to over 1,600 transmission structures, 6,637 broken poles, 2,926 transformers, and 338 miles of lines down. And this is just one of our power companies! They had to rebuild the entire electrical grid that could take at least six to eight weeks to get power.

As we drove into our city for the first time after the storm that next afternoon, the devastation from this disaster took our breath away. Tears flowed down our cheeks, and our mouths hung wide open in shock at what our eyes saw. It reminded me of the book of Lamentations, which describes a city in ruins. There was nothing left to do but weep. We made it to the street our home is on, and over forty pine trees were down across the road, making it impassable. It looked like a war zone. We stopped and got out to walk through and around the fallen trees to make it to our home. The debris and aftermath from this massive storm have changed the landscape forever.

FOR THE NEXT FOUR DAYS, I CRIED A LOT. THE OVERWHELMING THOUGHTS OF WHERE TO START CLEANING UP AFTER SOMETHING LIKE THIS CROWDED MY THOUGHT PROCESS.

Our home lost most of its roofing shingles, and plywood was exposed in some areas. The outside of our home was covered in debris, and the wood and siding were missing huge chunks. A few windows busted, and two massive trees laid beside it within feet of crushing our home completely. A dozen other trees laid down or bent in half. Ants were everywhere; they were disrupted too and scrambling to make a new home. Most families had giant trees either in their homes or lying on top of their homes, crushing the roof and beams below. Roofs that lost so many shingles exposing the bare plywood caused so much water damage as a gully washer came in not even twenty-four hours after the storm before anyone could tarp their homes. The ceilings caved in from the weight of the water in the insulation. The sounds of chainsaws and generators filled the air as people everywhere cleared paths to their homes. My husband and his father cut through over twenty pine trees. He pushed them off with an excavator to clear a path on the road for our neighbors and us to get our vehicles in our driveways.

The feeling of God abandoning us or that there's no hope because of what our eyes were trying to comprehend was such a lonely and desperate place. I know that God was with us, and everything passes by Him, but what I was feeling and seeing felt like desolation and despair. The grieving of our old life, our old home, and our memories were shouting louder than the thoughts that God loves us and God is with us. I felt as if the wind had been sucked out of my sails, and I was out in the middle of an ocean trying to keep my head above the water! I sat on our back porch probably on day three or four after Laura and wept violently. I wept because of the unknown. I wept because of the hopelessness taking over my mind. I wept because it felt impossible to bounce back from this storm. I wept because I felt like we were in a doom and gloom sappy story with our house situation. I wept because it did not feel fair. I wept because I was mad. I wept because I couldn't stop crying and felt overwhelmed. I wept because I was done. I had nothing else to give. I couldn't see into the future, and what I could see felt impossible and unbearable.

But in the eye of the storm, the GREAT I AM IS THERE! He is the calm that surrounds us. He is the stillness. He is the one that sees it all and holds us as we cry and shake uncontrollably. He knows the future, sees the bigger picture, and knows what needs to happen for His Power to be revealed and exposed.

God led a friend to check on me via text shortly after my mental breakdown weeping episode on our porch. With spotty cell service, I was able to type it all out and to tell her I felt helpless. She asked me to BELIEVE and not give up on God! She kept telling me this was His opportunity for His glory and power to be revealed! I pulled up my big girl pants, dried my eyes, and looked up. With nothing left in me I stared into the sky and told God, "I trust you. I don't understand, but I trust you. All I see is damaged destruction and devastation, but I trust you, Father."

After that moment, God sent me encouragement in so many ways. He sent my sister and friends in our direction to physically get hugs, hot meals, and things like rubber boots, mosquito spray, fans, water, tarps, work gloves, first aid kits, DampRid®, espresso shots, and other goodies! The love poured out on us was beautiful in so many ways. And what seemed like an impossible situation with our home turned out to be a way for us to see God's faithfulness and hand in our lives come into fruition.

This book is a collection of stories of women and their storms of life they witnessed and saw God's hand to discover His purpose for their lives. I pray these stories touch you and inspire you to dig deeper with Jesus and find His purpose for you in your life's storms.

Each story has a devotional section at the bottom for you to press into the Holy Spirit and grow deeper with God. Sometimes we'll never understand why our storms in life come in and tear us down, but we can look to our God because He loves us.

HE CAN TURN WHAT WAS MEANT FOR OUR MISERY INTO A GREAT AND MIGHTY GIFT TO USE FOR HIS PURPOSE.

ANCHOR MY SOUL

CHAPTER ONE

AWARENESS OF
WHAT'S BREWING
jessica turner

For as long as I can remember, I've lived life behind forced smiles. My life appeared to be the image of perfection from the bystander looking in when in reality it was only a charade saturated in hopelessness. When the cost of that charade threatened my life, I finally faced the truth. I was sinking, and I was sinking fast.

I was six months postpartum with my twin girls, and I struggled to find a thread of hope to hang on to. For months, I had been told by other twin moms that *this* was just normal; I was in the most demanding season there is. Yet, I just couldn't shake this feeling that what I was walking through wasn't "normal," even as a twin mom.

Some days it would take all I had to get out of bed, to break away from the daydream of going back to the me I used to know - before becoming a mother. I struggled with loving them the way they deserved and recognized hidden resentment towards those closest to me. I wanted so badly to love this new life I had been blessed with, especially since it had been such a long road to get here, but I just couldn't, and the guilt was crippling.

I KNEW I NEEDED TO GET HELP, AND I FINALLY DID.

I still remember that day like it was yesterday. I snuck away to our surgery room (I was a veterinarian at this point in my story) to call my doctor and told her that I thought I was struggling with postpartum depression. Just saying the words out loud was so freeing, as if a tremendous weight had been lifted from my shoulders. But it was also embarrassing. I had always seen this transparency as a sign of weakness as an indicator that I was doing something wrong as not only a person but also a mother. I felt like a total failure, a fraud, saying I didn't have it all together. I now recognize why so many remain in silence, even if it doesn't ultimately cost them their lives.

I wish that would have been the end of my struggle with PPD, but it wasn't. It was just the beginning of what felt like a total dismantlement of everything I ever knew, followed by the most beautiful, unexpected story of restoration.

I thought that I could just take a little pill every day and the old me would emerge, ready to be the mother I always dreamed of being. Once again, I was wrong, and that realization led to even more profound despair. Luckily, I had a doctor who took the time to sit with me as a friend and her patient. I still say she was one of the many angels God placed in my path during that season. She loved me enough to help me see the hard truth of where I was, and it required work on my end to get out of it. I needed to take care of myself. While that initially looked like making time to work out and eat healthily, it ultimately led to a deeper relationship with God.

I had honestly never experienced a relationship, as I had been guilty of just going through the motions but never stopping and inviting Jesus in. I found a new source of hope, unwavering and able to sustain me no matter what I was facing. A hope I would desperately need to cling on to as I continued to peel back the layers of my past and the mountains I would be asked to climb soon.

The deeper I dug into knowing Christ, the more I saw myself through His eyes. I finally identified pieces of my story pushed down for decades, knowing I wasn't facing them alone this time.

I opened my eyes to my struggling with disordered eating from an early age. Many of my battles with food, self-worth/image, and acceptance were birthed within that period of my life.

I came to recognize that anxiety and depression have not been a new chapter in my story but one woven in most of my life.

I revisited a time in my life completely blotted out until recently because of my inability to cope. Someone close decided that the demands of life and veterinary school were too much for her to bear. A life temporarily spared due to my discovery of her attempt to end her life that morning.

Until she succeeded in her attempt at suicide this past summer of 2019, I never processed what happened on that day or the scars it left. While we weren't as close as we were when it all began, the validation of her hopelessness sent me on a path I wasn't ready to travel. One that forced me to relive every little detail from that day, along with the depth of my trauma due to never properly healing from it.

I honestly think I will never "get over" her death, but I continue to move forward in confidence, knowing that Jesus is by my side every step of the way. He is waiting to be my source of everything in the next mountain I'll climb.

NOW I SMILE NOT AS A FACADE OF THE PERFECT LIFE BUT BECAUSE I HAVE FOUND A JOY THAT IS UNSHAKEABLE IN HIM.

DEVOTION
andrea bourgeois

Awareness of where we are in Christ is vital for us to survive this life, especially in trials and tribulations.

When the chatter and rumors of two hurricanes coming in our direction began, every momma in the path of the storm did a mental check for:

Do we have plenty of water? Where's the generator? Do we have batteries? Baby food? Diapers? Snacks and canned foods? Where are we going to go if it gets worse? Will we need to board the windows and doors? Is it heading straight for us? Medicines - do we have everything we need?

It's part of our gut instinct to think ahead and plan for the worst-case scenario in our minds whether we voice the concerns out loud or not. We have to assess and know where we stand in all the preparations.

Awareness of where we are with Christ and what's happening around us is vital for the rest of our survival steps to be accomplished. How can we reach out for help without the awareness we need help?

To assess and know where we are to heal physically, emotionally, and spiritually is the first step. Identifying issues, heartaches, struggles, weaknesses, sin, and strongholds takes time but is crucial for proper healing.

We need to acknowledge our struggle and our need for God to reveal the root for us to work towards healing. If we don't have wisdom in an area, the Bible tells us to ask for it, and it's given to us. God wants us to ask for instructions and His direction out of our mess. He'll guide us out through the Holy Spirit.

We need to know what's brewing out in the waters so we can be prepared. We need awareness of where we are in Christ, so He can lead us to calmer water and safer ground.

Are you aware of your struggles and weaknesses? Do you see how your habits and thought processes create a storm from within that will only strengthen over time? Do you recognize the forces against you and our enemy's tactics? Can you identify the root or stronghold that's holding you back?

FOR THE EARTH WILL BE FILLED WITH THE KNOWLEDGE OF
THE GLORY OF THE LORD AS THE WATERS COVER THE SEA.

Habakkuk 2:14

IF ANY OF YOU LACKS WISDOM, LET HIM ASK GOD,
WHO GIVES GENEROUSLY TO ALL WITHOUT REPROACH,
AND IT WILL BE GIVEN HIM.

James 1:5

THE FEAR OF THE LORD IS THE BEGINNING OF
KNOWLEDGE; FOOLS DESPISE WISDOM AND INSTRUCTION.

Proverbs 1:7

AND I WILL ASK THE FATHER, AND HE WILL GIVE YOU
ANOTHER COUNSELOR TO BE WITH YOU FOREVER - THE
SPIRIT OF TRUTH. THE WORLD CANNOT ACCEPT HIM
BECAUSE IT NEITHER SEES HIM NOR KNOWS HIM. BUT YOU
KNOW HIM, FOR HE LIVES WITH YOUR WILL BE IN YOU.

John 14: 16-17

CHAPTER TWO

— BUILD AN —
ARK
erin todd

My story is about insecurity, disordered eating, perfectionism, and a lifelong hustle for worthiness. But my story is not over yet. The latest chapter includes a spiritual awakening which has shown me my security comes from God and my worthiness is inherent.

Before this dawn, there was a dark night of dieting.

My issues with food and body image began in puberty. I didn't look like the other girls in middle school and couldn't fit into the clothes they wore, so I didn't "fit in". I certainly didn't look like the tall blonde girls I saw in magazines and on TV.

After absorbing the messages from school and society, I concluded I wasn't good enough. I believed I needed to change—specifically change my body—to become good enough. Thus began my decades of dieting.

From middle school to law school and well into my married years, I've tried every diet. I've worn every pant size. I've tried every exercise program. I've been up, then down, then back up. It's been an all-consuming roller-coaster ride.

Towards the end of the ride, I was so strict that I was orthorexic. You could say I had an unhealthy obsession with healthy eating.

There were months where I didn't think of anything else besides "health." My mind was continually doing the math of what I would eat that day, what I needed to meal prep for the rest of the week, how I would fit in my workouts, and what I expected my weigh-in to be at the end of the week.

I was totally invested in diet culture's values. I was certain all this health perfectionism was making me a better, more valuable person.

I was blinded by the false gospel of weight loss, promising me I could save myself and have the happy life I always wanted if I could just eat less and work harder. I was so blind; I couldn't see that dieting and "health" had become an idol.

At the height of my obsession, something unexpected happened. I not only hit my weight loss goal, but I also exceeded it. But I still wasn't happy.

Thanks to all the disordered behaviors I used to get there, I wasn't healthy either.

This surprised and confused me, unlike anything I had ever experienced. I realized I had been deceived by the lies of diet culture. Skinny does not equal happy. Thin does not equal healthy. I could finally see the truth for myself.

This revelation made me question my motives. Why did I want to lose weight in the first place? What did I really want? What did I think weight loss would give me? Happiness, confidence, security, peace, the life I've always dreamed of—that's what I thought it would give me. That's why it was such a shock when I hit my weight loss goal and I still didn't have those things.

I was only operating on the surface for all those years, thinking weight loss was about "feeling confident" or being my "best self". When I dug down deep the root cause was exposed. I believed weight loss was what I needed to be: safe, lovable, and valuable.

So, when I wanted to lose weight, what I really wanted was to feel good enough. What I really wanted was for someone to tell me I was unique, chosen, and important.

WEIGHT LOSS COULDN'T GIVE ME THOSE THINGS.
WEIGHT LOSS DIDN'T GIVE ME THOSE THINGS.

I had to lose the weight and still be unsatisfied to realize that I looked for satisfaction in the wrong place. I looked for that feeling of love and belonging to come from my appearance when it can only come from God.

To be loved, protected, valued, chosen, and feel like you belong—you don't have to lose weight to feel that way. That love is available to you right now from Jesus. You just have to accept it.

So, I accepted it all over again, but more thoroughly this time. With eyes of faith, I could see that what I really wanted was already here, waiting for me in Jesus, so I didn't need to diet anymore.

I was a slave to skinny until Jesus set me free.

I've stepped off the scale and stepped out in faith. Now I am pursuing well-being, not weight loss.

By His grace, I'm sharing the good news of the biggest life lesson I ever had to learn the hard way: weight loss is not the answer, Jesus is the answer.

By His redeeming love, what used to be an idol for me—health, food, and body—is now something that I use to glorify God.

Through His redeeming and transformative work on this lifelong idol, the Lord has turned my mess into my message and called me to serve my sisters who are stuck where I once was.

The Lord lit a fire in my heart to help women heal from the wounds of diet culture and discover, as I have, that their weight is not their worth. I am dedicated to showing women the better way the Lord showed me: intuitive eating. I like to call it the faith-fueled, freedom-filled, abundant life after dieting.

Letting go of diet culture's worldly wisdom and embarking on a new path towards true health has made me feel like a pioneer. Rejecting diets and the thin ideal is counter cultural at its core. But I trust His ways are higher. That's why I follow Jesus, not diets.

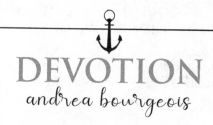

DEVOTION
andrea bourgeois

Do you believe the lies culture has illuminated and made enticing? Are you sinking in an area of your life? Has God called you to step out in faith and do something those around you don't understand? Can you trust God with the sin, the thought, the struggle, the lie, or what keeps you up at night and steals your joy throughout your day? Do you believe God has better for you?

I bet people thought Noah was crazy as he built the ark in faith. God sets us apart even when we are neck-deep in our struggles. Our past or our wrong mindset doesn't stop God's plans. Trust Him as He brings you back and provides a new beginning.

SOMETIMES GOD CALLS US TO DO SOMETHING BIGGER THAN WE CAN IMAGINE.

He sees us drowning in the lies from our culture and knows our hearts want His way, yet we can't find our way there. Our struggle has us in a vast ocean on the brink of sinking alongside everyone else, but God knows our potential and how He created us. He calls us out of the deep waters and tells us to build an ark. He knows the destruction that's coming, and He provides a way out or a new beginning.

He has a job assignment for us. He wants to reprogram our brains by taking a massive leap of faith in trusting His way is the BEST way.

God is in the business of restoration and healing after major storms and trials. The only way to reach full recovery with Jesus is to allow Him to take over our heart and mind. Sometimes He must take us back to where it all started to expose the lies that have held us down. God will peel back the layers to speak life and truth if we are willing and able.

"BUT NOAH FOUND FAVOR IN THE EYES OF THE LORD."
"SO, MAKE YOURSELF AN ARK OF CYPRESS WOOD; MAKE
ROOMS IN IT AND COAT IT WITH PITCH INSIDE AND OUT."

Genesis 6:8,14

"FOR MY THOUGHTS ARE NOT YOUR THOUGHTS, NEITHER
ARE YOUR WAYS MY WAYS." DECLARES THE LORD. "AS THE
HEAVENS ARE HIGHER THAN THE EARTH, SO ARE MY WAYS
HIGHER THAN YOUR WAYS AND MY THOUGHTS THAN YOUR
THOUGHTS."

Isaiah 55:8-9

ANCHOR MY SOUL

CHAPTER THREE

SHELTER IN
THE STORM
chelsey dematteis

Looking back on those years of running through rebellion, I see a girl who wanted nothing more than to be pursued. My heart yearned for wholeness yet didn't understand that wholeness was found in the One who created me. Underneath each area of pain in my story, you'd find the lie tucked away; however, I was too broken and too messy to see an escape from my patterns of sin.

Not so long ago, I found myself deep in prayer, asking The Lord where my rebellion stemmed from. When did the brokenness entangle my heart? Who sowed the seed? I wasn't a textbook rebellious girl. My issues didn't stem from a lacking in my dad's affection. It was quite the opposite. My dad has always been in my corner. Rooting for me, supporting me, always telling me how beautiful, capable, kind, and gifted I am. This issue with worth, value, and love just wasn't making sense.

Then Lord revealed this to my heart, "Chelsey, it's nothing that was done to you and nothing you did to someone; it's what you saw." He led me back to my seven-year-old self sitting on the carpet in the back room at a family member's house. Then I saw it. MTV spring break plastered on the TV. I saw the girl dancing on stage in her brown two-piece bikini, selling her innocence to the world for all to see.

At that moment, sin planted a seed. The seed was sown through my eyes and slithered into my heart. A seed that then continued to be watered by the world and its never-ending desire to pervert the truth. The enemy latched onto this image and wanted nothing more than for me to set my gaze on this false feeling. Satan deceived me into believing a young woman needed to act like the girl on TV to be loved, pursued, and desired.

The Lord then took me to Matthew 6:22-23, "The eye is the lamp of the body. So, if your eye is healthy, your whole body will be full of light, but if your eye is bad, your whole body will be full of darkness. If then the light in you is darkness, how great is the darkness."

This seed of deception and darkness spiraled into the awful storms that come with rebellion. I found myself in the raging seas of giving myself away in ways God never desired of me. I was led down the long road of eating issues. My heart was broken as I struggled with body image. Soon, I was plagued with anxiety that became never-ending.

Rebellion does this. It shackles us and fills us with fear. It has drastic twists and turns in the road attached to all the emotion led choices. It grabs hold of our hearts and steals other parts of who we are. Rebellion creates chaos in the very place The Lord designed to be sacred. This is what rebellion was doing to me. Shackling me, filling me with fear, and leading me astray in false feelings.

In the Spring of my freshman year at college, The Lord showed up as my rescuer. This became my rescue story. The campus police showed up in my dorm parking lot. They handed me a golden ticket, a ticket to see them in court in two weeks for underage consumption and open container. Some may not see this as a golden moment in my life, but for me, this was the moment I noticed God intersect my mess undeniably. He used this moment to light up my path, and His light pierced my heart.

God began the amazing work of redemption and healing from this moment on in my life. He took my places of pain and gave them purpose. He showed me He loved me where I was but loved me too much to leave me unchanged. He opened my eyes to see what a good Father He is and that He was always in pursuit of me. My heart became filled with the truths that I was chosen, loved, redeemed, found, and bought with a price. I believed for the first time that Jesus went to the cross for me.

I felt a blanket of security, knowing that not one moment of my life was hidden from Him. God saw all my peaks and valleys; He was there for all of them yet loved me anyway. He understood the cries of my heart. He was there the moment the seed of deception was sowed and made it His mission to bring my heart home no matter how much sin I was entangled in.

When I surrendered my life to Him, I saw that there is always an escape for those in Christ, and His word concreted that for me. 1 Corinthians 10:13, "No temptation has overtaken you that is not common to man. God is faithful, and he will not let you be tempted beyond your ability. Still, with the temptation, he will also provide the way of escape, that you may be able to endure it."

He will give a way of escape to those who love Him. He will lead, love, and usher us out of the pits. He is faithful and always truthful. My life attests to that. By His grace and mercy over my life, He shattered the sinful seed that was planted all those years ago. What the enemy meant for evil, God has used to write a beautiful redemption story. He showed me that no one is too dirty, too broken, or too tainted to receive the love of Christ and the truth of the gospel. He saves, redeems, and writes the story for His glory. If He calmed the raging storm in Galilee, He will calm and redeem the raging storms inside of you and me.

DEVOTION
andrea bourgeois

God always provides safety and protection when we are in harm's way. Scripture tells us we'll never be tempted beyond what we can handle! I remember watching the weather channel and local news while waiting anxiously to see what Laura would do out in the gulf. Was she going to gain strength and be as strong as Rita was in 2005? As the days went by, the storm grew as it collided with the low pressure. God provided an outlet for us to be safe and evacuate to the family who lived in Covington, LA. He moved us temporarily as the storm came through and provided His protection.

GOD WILL HIDE US IN HIS SHELTER IN THE DAY OF TROUBLE!

When we got home and saw the aftermath, there were moments where I honestly couldn't see how we'd overcome this catastrophe. But I kept thinking, no matter what - God won't abandon us, and He won't give us anything we can't handle. He's provided shelter for us not only when we evacuated but also little things or blessings that encouraged us to keep going. His hand has been all around us throughout every step. He can be only faithful!

Our chaos can grow as it collides with more temptations and mess; we find ourselves trapped within our storm. The Lord allows us to get "caught" or "hit rock bottom" so we can look back to Him and regain our focus in this life.

Sometimes God allows things to happen even when living in His presence and "doing all the right things," as reading His word and aligning our life with His will. When hard things occur, and we feel abandoned, he can use the pain and hardship for His will and purpose. Maybe He lets it get us ready for what's coming ahead or to get out of something we are currently in because He has something better!

I know so many families are dealing with demolishing and gutting their homes to start all over from scratch because of the roof and water damage from Hurricane Laura. A friend said while passing out food at a church nearby a few days after the storm, "As devastating as it is to lose everything, the silver lining is I get the new interior remodel I've always wanted. We'd never be able to remodel if it weren't for Laura." God sometimes uses things like this for us to see His faithfulness that He'll always provide.

Are you running away from God? Or are you running away with God as your shelter in the storm? Can you see the silver lining?

God will always provide for us! We must keep our focus on Him and believe that He will pull through with a way because He's the ultimate WAY MAKER!

"NO TEMPTATION HAS OVERTAKEN YOU THAT IS NOT COMMON TO MAN. GOD IS FAITHFUL, AND HE WILL NOT LET YOU BE TEMPTED BEYOND YOUR ABILITY. STILL, WITH THE TEMPTATION, HE WILL ALSO PROVIDE THE WAY OF ESCAPE, THAT YOU MAY BE ABLE TO ENDURE IT."

1 Corinthians 10:13

ANCHOR MY SOUL

CHAPTER FOUR

EYES ON
JESUS
amy debrucque

I realized in recent years that I've always welcomed and encouraged others to share their burdens and pain. I was unwilling to be that vulnerable myself.

It's always been easier to offer a fresh perspective when it hasn't applied to my own life.

I've always been a private person, yet even during my worst times with anxiety, I never thought about offering that to anyone else. Considering myself to be a capable person, being that vulnerable was off the table. God's plans overruled anything I could have possibly imagined and turned my pain with anxiety into great purpose.

I laugh when I think about how hard God had to pursue me and was still willing to stay by my side. I took longer than most to finally pay attention to all the signs and signals He brought to my attention on how to move from living in fear of finding daily freedom.

On a random spring evening, I received a call from my mother that they had diagnosed my oldest brother with a brain tumor. I felt like my world had stopped. It was surreal. Until that point, life and death had been carried out in the assumed order. The news of my brother exposed more than his inevitable fate but also trust and control issues I had with God.

My first glimpse of that lack of control came after we immediately flew down to see my brother in the hospital the day after his diagnosis. He was tearfully telling my mom that he didn't care about what happened to him. His only concern was for his wife and son. My mother responded, like most would, to reassure her child that she wouldn't let anything happen to him.

At that moment, my heart immediately shattered because I knew her words weren't true. Our parents can't control and protect us from all things, good or bad.

I had been counting on earthly protection from my parents and even my eternal wellness. The solid ground I thought I had been standing on until that point immediately felt unsteady.

During my brother's diagnosis and final days, I got married and gave birth to my first child, a son named Alexander. He was a light in a dark time. Being a mother was a gift I dreamed about my entire life, and he was perfect. Most girls dream about big houses and prominent careers, but I always dreamt of being a mom.

Adjusting to motherhood was exhausting, but it was also a good distraction to my brother's failing health. It gave me permission to put aside the underlying fears that had seeped in.

Fifteen months after my brother's diagnosis, he passed away. While at his funeral, I still hadn't reconciled that God didn't answer our prayers to heal him on earth. Or face the truth that we couldn't have fixed him.

Returning home brought more sobering news with the unexpected death of my son. Two significant losses in 16 days. I was flattened, and the shaky ground I had been standing on had now caved in. Fear and anxiety took over.

I realized later that my foundation was weak because I thought my parents and I were the ones securing it. God would be the only one who could secure the future for my brother, my son, and for me.

I had always been a believer, but not always trusted. I wanted to live with God as my guide instead of the driver. The losses exacerbated my fear, but also my pride. I didn't want to ask for help, so I went on feeling lost, broken, and lonely. I was embarrassed about my anxiety struggle. It made me feel weak, and I did everything I could to overcome it on my own. I was using God as my support instead of the leading role of my healing.

I continued to move on with life and had four more healthy children. Yet, the private struggle remained.

I PRETENDED I WAS DOING GREAT.

I was so determined to fix myself that I didn't want anyone else to know any different. I did what most prideful people do; I faked it. I wanted to be doing better than I was, and I wasn't sure why it was taking me so long to figure it all out.

Lucky for me, God continued to chase me down. He finally presented me with a grand gesture that would get my attention. Right before my 40th birthday, I received a cancer diagnosis. Hodgkin's-Lymphoma.

It sounds crazy, but I was almost expecting it. I would never have prayed for it, but it gave me a sense of relief to finally surrender.

The cancer diagnosis ultimately saved my life. The past 15 years had been gripped with fear, and now I had the chance to let it go and be free. I remember getting down on my knees to pray and hearing God ask if I would trust Him now.

I immediately said "Yes. I surrender."

Surrendering all my fears to God was the missing piece that fit perfectly with the other practices to help with my anxiety.

Surrendering gave me control. Not over God's plan for my future, but over my fear. My relationship with Him is restored, and I find purpose in everything.

Anxiety and fear are joy stealers. I missed so much because of my distracted mind I am now driven to make a daily choice to surrender. I remind myself fear is normal, but courage gets the final say.

I learned that the life I want to live is on the other side of fear, and that's where God is always waiting for me.

DEVOTION
andrea bourgeois

God is the constant peace we are so desperately searching for in this life. Sometimes He calls us out into deep waters to trust Him when the ocean rises around us. Grief, fear, and anxiety can keep us in the boat afraid as we watch the storms approach us feeling vulnerable and exposed.

Jesus didn't say, "Peter, come!" He said, "Come!" He calls us all out of the safety boat in our storms to walk on the raging sea with Him!

As soon as Peter allowed doubt and fear to take over his mind, he sank. Jesus was right there to extend His hand and catch him. Jesus is right beside us. As soon as we cry out to Him, He extends His grace, His mercy, His love, His presence, and His peace immediately in our time of need.

Where are you in your relationship with Christ? Are you sitting in the boat afraid? Are you ready to take that leap of faith out of the boat and meet Him on the raging waters? Are you seeing and observing the surrounding wind causing fear to distract you instead of keeping your eyes focused on Jesus? Are you sinking and can't keep your head above the waves?

God is our everlasting peace in chaos. He is calling us out to the deep water to trust Him! When our eyes are fixed on Him, we can do the impossible with Him guiding and leading the way.

JESUS SENT HIS DISCIPLES AHEAD OF HIM AS HE DISMISSED THE CROWDS AFTER FEEDING THE THOUSANDS BEFORE DARK AND WENT UP ON THE MOUNTAINSIDE BY HIMSELF TO PRAY. WHEN JESUS WENT OUT TO THEM IN THE FOURTH WATCH, ROUGHLY 3AM - 6AM, THE DISCIPLES HAD BEEN ROWING AGAINS STRONG WINDS FOR OVER TWELVE HOURS AND
THEN SAW HIM WALKING TOWARDS THEM ON THE WATER AND WERE TERRIFIED.

THEY THOUGHT HE WAS A GHOST AND CRIED OUT IN FEAR! JESUS IMMEDIATELY SAID TO THEM, "TAKE COURAGE! IT IS I. DON'T BE AFRAID."

PETER REPLIED, "IF IT IS YOU LORD, TELL ME TO COME TO YOU ON THE WATER." JESUS SAID, "COME." THEN PETER GOT DOWN OUT OF THE BOAT AND WALKED ON THE WATER TOWARD JESUS. BUT WHEN PETER SAW THE WIND, HE WAS AFRAID AND BEGAN TO SINK AND CRIED OUT, "LORD, SAVE ME!" IMMEDIATELY JESUS REACHED OUT HIS HAND AND CAUGHT PETER. JESUS SAID, "YOU OF LITTLE FAITH, WHY DID YOU DOUBT?"

THEY CLIMBED INTO THE BOAT AND THE WIND INSTANTLY DIED DOWN.

Matthew 14:22-33

CHAPTER FIVE

-PERSEVERANCE-
stephanie broersma

The catalysts for our brokenness don't always result in suffering and tears, although I've shed gallons worth of salty emotions. Difficulty and heartaches come in all sizes shaping our lives, resulting in us burying the pain somewhere deep inside, hindering our perspective and camouflaging blessings. The Enemy wins when we can't see the face of Jesus while worshiping Him through the shattered mess of our everyday brokenness.

My mess began in sixth grade when the bitter, somber word, cancer, entered our family's vocabulary. A noun that later entangled itself in multiple family member's feeble frames, and eventually, choking out life unwilling to surrender to the disease.

Psalm 32:7 has been a prayer through much of my mess. "You are my hiding place; you will protect me from trouble and surround me with songs of deliverance." I pleaded with God to spare my Dad's health so I'd have him alive to walk me down the aisle at my wedding. Moments before the church doors opened, with perfect make-up applied threatening to smear as tears fell down my cheeks, I stood beside my Dad on my marriage day. Little did I know the vows spoken that day would be in question seven years later, as my husband's sin would take our marriage hostage under the spell and devastating web of pornography.

My husband sat me down and confessed to a ten year pornography addiction that led to multiple physical affairs. Our existence as a couple was scattered with deceit and secrets; our marriage bed shared with strangers. He wept as the ugly truth he had been hiding from me for years, was finally set free. The Enemy—no longer in control to silence my husband of the filthy sin—shuddered as Truth was now invited into our horribly broken marriage.

Yet on this day, the day my marriage died, my sister received results showing her breast cancer (diagnosed just two years earlier) had stopped spreading. It was a day to celebrate; not a day to grieve. I struggled to sleep or eat; the couch became my bed for weeks after the confession. My Mom held me as the tears found no shut off switch; the weight of reality crippling me from any parental responsibilities. The details of the betrayal tormented my soul.

Psalm 77 is defined by troubling self-reflection, draped with temptation and darkness. The Psalmist finds himself in such need he was physically stretched out with his hand laid before the Lord crying out to God for comfort and mercy. Paralyzed by fear for our future, I too, had hands outstretched begging God to take the pain away. I asked God why He allowed this to happen within our marriage. I was angry, embarrassed, feeling shame for my husband's sins, violated by the filth which entered his mind and slipped past his hands. The night of confession I tried washing off the disgust that now wore me like an article of clothing; my arms bleeding from scrubbing under the scorching hot water. There were moments of yelling at God for what I was experiencing; complaining about my situation and complete brokenness. Then, much like the Psalmist, I had an awakening which translated my fears into hope. It happened when I stepped backed and remember what God had done and was doing in my life. God's promises and works He was doing became a sanctuary of hope on some of the hardest days of my life. The "but then" is a critical part of our brokenness. (Psalm 77:10-14) It's the point of transition from sorrow to joy. The point we see our dire need for God verses being stuck in our pity and ashes.

Fast forward five years, my husband and I, with ugly cry and sand between our toes, renewed our vows taking all the brokenness within our marriage promising better; giving God rights to our entire lives. The blessing of new beginnings. Brokenness is a matter of surrendering control of our life to God, releasing the best laid out plans for His will. Throughout the many messes I had experienced, God had been building a blessing resume in my life. One that would carry me through another devastating moment in my life; another moment to surrender to God. I never left my sister's side in the hours leading to her passing away after fighting with such incredible vigor to a disease which had consumed her entire essence, dreams and her life. Never will I forget her hand—humble, loving, and serving— go limp in mine. My spirit left shattered. All I could do is weep; grief devoured me.

But then, I remembered the wonders of my broken journey and found myself with the only option left with... to worship through the fractured, beautiful mess. To bring before God all the mess regardless how hollow I felt; forcing myself to see the greater glory and joy in my earthly pain. Psalm 126:5 tells us, "Those who sow in tears will reap with songs of joy." God has returned joy in my life. I've learned to process grief through desperate worship as my husband and I painfully sowed tears, restoring our now thriving marriage. My Dad still wraps his familiar arms around me as a testament to blessings of physical healing, and I see glimpses of my sister in the fluttering of a hummingbird or promise in a rainbow. God continues to sustain me, allowing the blessings to flow, as I surrender the mess through my broken worship. My brokenness can easily be summed up by Rick Warren who shares, "The deepest level of worship is praising God in spite of the pain, thanking God during a trial, trusting Him when tempted, surrendering while suffering and loving Him when He seems distant."

As long as I have breath, I will continue to worship.

DEVOTION
andrea bourgeois

Rejoicing in the storm gives our authority back over to Jesus to release His power and hand in our life. He sees us thank Him even though we are suffering and can't see beyond our pain. We know with full confidence He is with us and He's got a plan. Rejoicing and worshiping Him with our praise in our storms keeps our focus on Him and not our circumstances. God will use our pain to mold us into who He has created us to be. He's going to push out the old in us and replace it with Him. When we persevere in a storm, we are changed from the inside out. When our hearts are focused on God above, our attitudes and mindset change and reflect more of Him, and our hope grows stronger. The hope God gives us in the storm is indescribable because it's poured out by the Holy Spirit. It's given to us by the supernatural power of God. We can't describe it and sometimes we can't understand it, but we know we have it to hang on to daily.

Are you in the middle of your storm? Have you taken a moment to praise Him in it, to thank Him for it, or to worship Him because of it?

Our God is good Father. In the storms of life, it's hard to see His goodness because of the pain we feel and experience. Trust Him to reveal more of Himself to you and ask Him to change you in it. Ask Him to help you persevere and be molded into who He has created you to be. He's there ready to make a difference. Are you?

"NOT ONLY SO, BUT WE ALSO REJOICE IN YOUR
SUFFERINGS, BECAUSE WE KNOW THAT SUFFERING
PRODUCES PERSEVERANCE; PERSEVERANCE PRODUCES,
CHARACTER; AND CHARACTER, HOPE. AND HOPE
DOES NOT PUT US TO SHAME, BECAUSE GOD'S
LOVE HAS BEEN POURED OUT INTO OUR HEARTS
THROUGH THE HOLY SPIRIT, WHO HAS BEEN
GIVEN TO US."

Romans 5:3-5

CHAPTER SIX

ANCHOR
OF HOPE
lindsey bett

Have you ever had something spoken to you that altered your life? A moment that changed your life forever. My husband and I have.

In 2003, doctors gave us devastating news about our two-year-old son, Joel. Your son is in heart failure. He has an incurable, very rare, life-threatening disease called Pulmonary Hypertension. For an overview, PH is a lung disease, and it has no cause. It restricts the pulmonary vessels, and since the heart and lungs work together, it doesn't allow the heart to get the right blood and oxygen it needs. Thus, causing right heart failure.

What followed was a two-night stay at a local hospital until he was stable enough to be flown to a more experienced hospital. We weren't allowed to fly with him, so I watched in agony as my baby was being flown without me. I thought that was the hardest thing I would ever do. Time would reveal that wasn't the case. At this new hospital, we were given more bad news, and after more tests, we were told he was the worst case they had ever seen, and they didn't know how to properly treat him. After an agonizing month there and pleading with God for his life, we were told he needed a lung transplant and would be sent to a larger hospital to get further care. Our family had no prior medical experience. This world was so new and overwhelming to us.

Now, my son was being flown to another hospital. We were grateful once we arrived because the doctors were more educated and experienced in his diagnosis. They assured us he did not need a transplant, but only needed to change up his meds. He had surgery that left him with a central line that was placed into his heart with external access to receive 24-hour life-sustaining medicine through a pump. The doctors informed us we would take on a doctor and pharmacist's role in his care. If we wanted to return home, we would need training to mix his medicine. This process would take about thirty minutes every other day. Any improper mixing of this process could cause severe and life-threatening complications for him. Along with three to four times a day oral med. No pressure!

After six weeks of being in the hospital, we were discharged! And what a great homecoming it was. We were finally able to be reunited as a family. We have two older boys. Reuniting with his brothers was the best therapy for Joel! Life as we knew it was flipped upside down. To keep Joel from getting sick, I now had to homeschool our two other boys. After only two months, Joel declined again. His heart failure was worsening at a rapid pace. We faced more devastating news. The doctor said he thought Joel would have only six months to a year to live without a heart and double lung transplant. Another kick to the gut. We prayed so many prayers and started our research. We learned the lung is the most rejected organ in the body—more bad news. But we kept praying and contacted another specialist for a second opinion.

We met with a new doctor known worldwide for his expertise in my son's condition. He thought he had a little more time after reviewing his case and didn't need the transplants just yet. We switched our care to him and his team. He was sent by God to us because we had hope for the first time in a long time. And he would fight with us for our child. But Joel continued to steadily decline. We were presented with the option of a new exploratory surgery that could give his heart relief. Still, it was only done on less than ten children in the US. More agonizing prayer took place. But then we knew this was the route to take. He would have this risky surgery. Remember when I mentioned leaving my son to fly alone without me was the hardest thing ever? No, holding my son and praying over him right before he was wheeled off for this surgery was the most challenging moment of my life. He made it through the surgery and a painful recovery, but he did great.

A few weeks after surgery, I was cooking dinner and heard Joel running around the house. This was something Joel could not do in the past; his body couldn't handle it. I was blown away and immediately grabbed my phone to document this miracle!

Has this all played out like I would like? Not at all. Joel still has a severe PH. If it were up to me, he would have been fully healed in his hospital bed. But I'm not God. He loves Joel more than I do, and I trust His plans for our lives. We have seen God's hand every step of the way. Our lives have never been the same, but that's not always in the negative sense. Yes, there have been plenty of horrible days: tears, pain and suffering, questioning, and Joel coming close to death many times. I've also walked through much anxiety, fear, PTSD, and depression. But there has been so much love, support, deeper faith, watching God do miracles, grow others' faith, and more positives than I can count.

We aren't promised a trouble-free life on this earth. But we are promised that God would be with us through it all, no matter what devastating news we may have been given.

DEVOTION
andrea bourgeois

The moment Christ died on the cross, the veil was torn in half to have direct access to our Father in heaven. The hope that Christ gives is given to us from behind the curtain. It's holy. It's supernatural. Jesus anchors us down in the waters in our storms and keeps us from floating away. We are anchored in love and are held in place regardless of what is happening around us. The hope Jesus gives us is surrounded in peace and in security.

Are you struggling with finding hope in your situation? Do you feel like you are drifting further away? Can you see the anchor of hope that God is offering?

IMAGINE GOD AS THE ANCHOR TO YOUR BOAT.

He is keeping you on track. He's provided stability and security in the storms that arise. The boat may get damaged, but He keeps you alive and still. He keeps you afloat right where He wants you.

Hope is what keeps us looking up and hanging on for supernatural strength when life seems unbearaable. The waters may surround us, but if we have Jesus, we can survive.

"WE HAVE THIS HOPE AS AN ANCHOR FOR
THE SOUL, FIRM AND SECURE. IT ENTERS THE INNER
SANCTUARY BEHIND THE CURTAIN."

Hebrews 6: 19

CHAPTER SEVEN

──GOD'S LOVE IS LIKE──
A HURRICANE
k. price

My experiences regarding rejection began as a young girl. Lunchtime was the best or worst time of my day. I remember in sixth grade when my best friends told me I couldn't sit with them. They "didn't like me anymore" and insisted I find a new table. These were my best friends since kindergarten and first grade. I was heartbroken. They didn't ask me to sit with them again for two years.

The rejection carried over into dating relationships.

I only dated one boy growing up, and that was a month after I graduated high school, but I had plenty of crushes. Every other week I liked someone new. When I expressed my affection, the crush of the week would respond by casually crumpling and discarding my "Will you go out with me?" note.

Rejection is apparently my expertise. I lived with it through high school, in college, and into adulthood. I was always "too something," for someone. I was too *white* for the black girls at school, but nowhere near *preppy* enough for the white girls. I was too *geeky* for the "skater" kids, but too *punk* for the "nerds." I'm a professional at not fitting in. I faced plenty of negative looks, dissolved friendships, and solo meals. Eventually, that rejection wore me down. When coming of age, I was adamant on not experiencing rejection ever again if I could help it. My goal in my college years was to be everyone's friend, no matter who I had to become.

It didn't take me long to experience rejection again, even though I was trying so hard to appease the world. It wore me down, so much so, I started to self-implode. I rejected my body, hated how I was created, and believed it had to be the reason I was so undesirable. I developed an eating disorder; overtraining and starving my body to regain some control over my life and my looks. I experimented with marijuana in high school, and immediately found a similar crowd in college to get high with. Almost every weekend I over consumed alcohol, but I felt these habits were to my advantage as they numbed my negative emotions and got me in the crowd I saw as cool and worthy. I titled myself as "The Rejection Queen." It was becoming a pattern that I would only hold the attention of a male for approximately two days before I was old news. This eventually led me to give up on boys and pursued dating relationships with girls instead. I figured to be so undesirable, I must have been searching in the wrong place the whole time, and likely was just meant to be with girls.

THAT ALL CHANGED WHEN I MET THE MAN WHO SAVED MY SOUL FOR ALL ETERNITY. JESUS.

For me to meet God, He saw it necessary to remove distractions from my line of vision. Through a series of events, both in and out of my control, He brought me to a place of long-suffering. I had no job and was living at my mother's house. With no car, no money, no drugs, and no friends, I was isolated and humble, living in my little brother's room.

I had been interested in the Christian faith and participated in a campus ministry during the spring semester. They left us with a summer reading challenge, and through reading Mark 4, the Parable of the Sower, I found I couldn't even begin to house the roots of spiritual growth and change in my life with the way I had been living. God brought me to my knees in repentance, accepting Jesus as my Savior and Living Water in my mother's living room. He began a good work of healing me from my sinful ways, and showed me how I was created in His beautiful image.

Psalm 139:14 and 2 Corinthians 4:16 would validate that God had created me perfectly, that I had a purpose for this earthly body, and these verses helped me to   continue to overcome my battle with eating disorders. 1 Peter 5:8 taught me the importance of being sober-minded as I stood at the watch gate for Christ's return. 1 Peter 2:4 would remind me that Christ, the cornerstone, experienced the ultimate rejection by his people and Father, so I wouldn't have to at the end of my days. Romans 10: 9-13 then sealed in me I was forever accepted by my Father in heaven, after I accepted His Son.

As the Alpha and the Omega, the beginning and the end, the only true way to heaven and intimacy with the Father, Jesus' rejection was far worse than anything I have ever felt in my short lifetime. However, it shows again one more way God in the flesh understands His creation. Jesus experienced the ultimate rejection. He was spat upon, flogged, beaten, and nailed to a wooden cross. His Father turned His face and rejected Him as He satisfied the sin sacrifice of the entire world. Jesus knows how rejection feels. Trust sister, that He can redeem your story of rejection too, and lead you to wholeness through his love for you.

DEVOTION
andrea bourgeois

DAVID CROWDER BAND'S SONG, "HOW HE LOVES US,"
WRITTEN BY JOHN MARK MCMILLIAN,
OPENS WITH THESE LYRICS:

HE IS JEALOUS FOR ME
LOVES LIKE A HURRICANE
I AM A TREE, BENDING BENEATH THE WEIGHT
OF HIS WIND AND MERCY...
IF HIS GRACE IS AN OCEAN, WE ARE ALL SINKING

Do you have thoughts, sins, or habits standing in the way between you and the God of the universe who created you?

Do you know how much God loves you?

Are you struggling to feel His presence?

Are you being isolated so you can hear God?

Close your eyes and feel the wind around you, He's there. Breathe in a deep breath, He's there. Imagine yourself as the tree and His love is as vast as hurricane and how His love engulfs you with each move. His love is grand. He made you so He can love you!

Our Father in Heaven loves us so much He wants all our focus on Him! When we place others, possessions, or ideas above Him, we allow the idols to take precedence over God in our lives. His love for us is so vast and greater than our minds can conceive.

I visualize us bending in the wind as His love makes landfall in our lives. He swoops in to get our attention, often knocking us down on our backs to where all we can do is look up at Him. Because God loves us, He will stop us in our tracks and create a time or period of isolation only to refocus us and to restore us on how He created us to be.

"Do not worship any other god,
for the Lord, whose name is
Jealous, is a jealous God."

Exodus 34:14

CHAPTER EIGHT

EYE OF THE
STORM

andrea bourgeois

I walked with suitcases hand in hand up my parent's driveway with the sunlight ricocheting off their tin roof as I watched the flowers disappear between the white picket fence. I was rehearsing my words repeatedly with that gut-wrenching stomachache forcing my body to shake and tremble. When I walked up the back stairs and opened the door, mom and dad were standing there. I couldn't get the words out. I just stood there and shrugged my shoulders as the tears streamed across my face. I was twenty-three years old. My life was slipping through my fingertips, and I could grasp none of it for the life of me. My marriage was over. I had nowhere else to go. All my dreams had shattered before my eyes, and the person I loved didn't want me any longer.

I WAS BROKEN. I WAS TORN.
I WAS EMBARRASSED.
I WAS AFRAID. I WAS LONELY.
I WAS SHATTERED TO MY CORE.

I laid many nights in my parent's guest room with my Bible, while tears streamed down my face. I was paralyzed. The pain in my heart was

63

unbearable on some days. That's when my mom took me running with her for the first time since I was a kid in a neighborhood not far from our house. I remember running with my iPod playing The David Crowder Band albums "Can You Hear Us?" and "Illuminate" on repeat. The pavement became my battlefield, where I poured out my heart to God. It was a release for my mind to run wild with the Lord, and somewhere between strides and roads that my feet touched, I met Jesus on a different level than I had known Him before.

Reading my Bible and the fundamentals of my relationship with Christ is what it is today because I got face-to-face with Him in my despair.

At the end of my Jesus years of restoration and discovering who God was molding me into, I went to Belize on a mission trip. One night the wind was picking up as I stood on the rooftop balcony overlooking the gulf coast. I stretched out my arms like Kate in Titanic. I stood with my eyes closed, feeling the wind run through my fingertips and my hair. I told the Lord right at that moment, "I TRUST YOU! I am ready for what's next!" I knew all the heartache and pain I'd experienced was needed so God could use me in a mighty way. He needed me to be this new version of me for what was ahead.

Within six months of my romantic Kate and Jack moment, I was falling in love with the man God had set aside just for me. Kindred spirits and patched up hearts with walls built for protection were melting for one another that summer. He was one of my dear friend's brother. Kerri had been trying to play match-maker for years, but she knew we both needed time to heal.

Brian and I married two years later Easter weekend with yellow flowers and lemons throughout my parents' new home's backyard and pergola. Now my sister-in-law had been diagnosed with rare liver cancer for over seven years. The year Brian and I got married began some painful chapters in my life. We watched her cancer deteriorate her earthen vessel over the next two years.

Our emotional roller coaster's ups and downs can't even be put into words to justify what our family went through. She left behind a husband, a son, a mom, a dad, a brother, a sister-in-law, and many friends and other

64

family members. The pain I watched and lived after her passing is so hard to describe to give it justice. The hole she left is indescribable. Grief came in like a storm brewing in the gulf only to sweep in for full destruction with us in its path. The hole in our family remains empty.

Sitting at a table setting boundaries and making amends was the least likely place we'd have thought our family would be two years after she was gone. Grief is ugly. It's raw. It's a real-life pain. But it's also where Jesus is ALIVE. It's also the place where our hearts are restored and renewed by His mighty power.

Those years of grief were also full of deep desires for Brian and me to become parents. The waiting period God allowed us to endure during those years pierced me directly in the heart with my hands tied behind my back. I remember getting to a place of desperation to become a mother, but what shifted my focus was when God posed the question, "Will you still love me even if the answer is no?" I had to search deep within my bones and love for the Lord to confidently and whole-heartedly say, "Yes, Lord. I will love and serve you with all my heart even if the answer is no." That was one of the most challenging seasons for me. The only way I could be joyful was to allow God to fill that void and to fill my heart with ALL of Him.

The following Easter weekend, I rode on the back of a gasoline motorized golf-cart with dust flying out behind the wheels as we winded down our sandy road to our condo. Brian and I had gone to this exact place on our honeymoon five years prior, but this time his mom and dad sat among us. I had loved Belize so much from my mission trip "titanic" experience, I convinced Brian to go for our honeymoon. And now, as our family of four had to relearn how to do life, we took a trip to celebrate the miraculous healing and restoration God did in our family. On a boat out in the most transparent bluest water I'd ever seen, I heard our family laugh again. It's incredible to witness God's power and faithfulness.

Again, the faithfulness and power of God were revealed and celebrated two months after our third trip to Belize with two blue lines on a stick. God is faithful. Our son is a constant reminder, He can do it AGAIN!

DEVOTION
andrea bourgeois

Our Heavenly Father is the eye of the storms of life as He is the "I AM" that is the center of lives, worlds, desires, needs, and futures. When the storms of life are raging, He is the peace in that chaos. In a hurricane, the wind and rain move in a counter clockwise motion creating an actual center of the storm that is calm without any wind or rain. The eye-wall, the inner most layer of the hurricane right next to the eye, is the most powerful and most destructive of all the winds. It demolishes anything in its path.

Our God is right next to us in the middle of whatever storm we find ourselves in within an arm's reach, with us falling apart and being knocked down. He allows the storms of life to occur because He knows how His love can be displayed through it, how His power will be used for His glory because of it, and how His mercy will be received after it.

God is our peace in the middle of our chaos. He is the calmness and stillness that our hearts and our souls crave.

Do you feel His blanket of peace over you? Can you see His hand in the chaos around you? Are you able to feel His presence when everything around is falling apart?

Cry out to our Lord and be still. Rest in His promises that He's our refuge and strength, an ever-present help in trouble.

"GOD IS OUR REFUGE AND OUR STRENGTH, AN EVER-
PRESENT HELP IN TROUBLE. THEREFORE WE WILL
NOT FEAR, THOUGH THE EARTH GIVE WAY AND THE
MOUNTAINS FALL INTO THE HEART OF THE SEA, THOUGH
ITS WATERS ROAR AND FOAM AND THE MOUNTAINS
QUAKE WITH THEIR SURGING."

"BE STILL AND KNOW THAT I AM GOD; I WILL BE EXALTED
AMONG THE NATIONS; I WILL BE EXALTED IN THE EARTH.
THE LORD ALMIGHTY IS WITH US; THE GOD OF JACOB IS
OUR FORTRESS."

Psalm 46: 1-3, 10-11

CHAPTER NINE

TOSSED BY THE
WAVES
Trudy Lonesky

Would you agree that our girls are struggling? They live in a filtered world of perfection, not realizing the images that leave them feeling unworthy are images of someone else's best day. Through social media and smartphones, our children are overwhelmed with feelings of comparison, self-doubt, and worthlessness. Anxiety, depression, and teen suicide are on the rise. Our call as mothers is urgent and the futures of our girls depend on us. Whether you have a teen/tween daughter of your own or you have influence over a girl in your life, God is calling us to rise.

One day while sitting in the passenger seat on our way back from a dance competition, my eleven-year-old daughter revealed to me that she would much rather compete on a dark stage at a competition than practice in a lighted room. In a lighted room, she can see faces, feel judgment, and assume what people in the room think about her and her performance. If left to her own wandering mind, she begins to feel like she doesn't measure up to the other dancers, compares her performance to them, and allows herself to feel defeated. On stage at a competition, it is completely dark. It's just her in the darkness, free to be herself, not worrying about what others think of her. There are no faces to read, no feelings of being judged, just her and the music, all alone.

I immediately thought about Genesis 3:11 when God asked Adam, "who told you, you were naked?" The serpent planted a seed of temptation to question God's goodness. The exact seed that affects humankind to this day.

Let's step back a little further to Genesis 3:1, "Now the serpent was more crafty than any of the wild animals the Lord God had made. He said to the woman, 'Did God really say, 'You must not eat from any tree in the garden.'"

At that moment, in the garden, the serpent gave Eve an open invitation to question God. That question would give Adam and Eve the idea that God and His plans and provisions over their lives weren't enough. Eve was tempted to believe God was withholding things from her and was invited to become separate and independent from God.

Who or what was it that began to chip away at my daughter's childlike faith? Who told her she wasn't enough? What made her feel like she needed to stay hidden in the dark? This challenged me to peel back the layers and consider where her past hurts began to sow seeds of self-doubt.

Even though we kept her from social media, it still found its way in her life. At nine years old, someone made a fake Instagram account in her name. At school, girls would take pictures of her, filter them in a nasty way, and upload them to Snapchat. She was teased, pushed, and tripped. She's been told she's not athletic, she stinks at anything she does, and she's not good enough. We don't lie in our house so she took these words as gospel in her little, impressionable heart. If people were saying these things, they must be true.

Soon all of this began to take its toll on her. In fourth grade, she would refuse to get out of our vehicle and go to school. The principal would have to come out to our car and remove her from it. I wasn't sure when or if I would see my girl be her funny, quirky, spunky self ever again.

Why God? It just didn't make sense. My fellow prayer warriors promised me through scripture that God would turn this all for good. That He had a special plan for her. That she was fearfully and wonderfully made, anointed, and highly favored. While in the midst of it, I couldn't see through the pain. Could there actually be any purpose in the suffering and burden she was carrying? How could this possibly turn to good?

BUT GOD....

God worked on my relationship with Him first. If I wanted my daughter to see herself as the beautiful creation God had made her to be, I needed to believe that for myself. If I am brutally honest, the reason I relate so much to teen girls and their searching is because at forty-two I was still searching to fill a deep pain within my own heart.

Past childhood hurts and rejections left me in a sea of unworthiness. As a child, I never felt good enough. I was made to feel like I was a mistake and unwanted. I was the poor kid, bullied most of my life. I carried these hurts all throughout my adult life, finding validation and worthiness in all the wrong places. I struggled with body image issues and sought approval from others.

God began a good work in me. He never intended for me to be able to fill my own longing for acceptance. If validation is filled by my own doing, I won't need God. God is the only One who will ever be able to completely fill that need. Where I find my identity will absolutely determine where my daughter finds her's.

God stood firm on His promise. He used the trials that my daughter faced to strengthen her. What the enemy meant for harm, God in fact turned to good. She no longer looks to the world for validation because it in those trials she leaned into God's truths and plans over her life. She is now able to decipher the enemy's lies and hold steadfast to God's word. She is a fierce warrior for God. Empowering and encouraging those around her to rebuke any lie the enemy has thrown their way.

Friend, we have Kingdom work to do. Our girls are under attack. We are under attack. But through it, we have an opportunity for a beautiful faith journey alongside our daughters- a renewing of our minds together.

DEVOTION
andrea bourgeois

In our storms, we will be tossed back and forth or blown here and there if we aren't careful where our focus is or who we are following. The people we surround ourselves with are the ones we vent to and seek help in our times of trouble. Are they God-fearing people? We need people to speak life into us when we are hurting and let us vent without judgment. We need godly advice and counsel because our enemy is out there looking for the next person to kill, steal, and destroy.

I had to learn early in my twenties that my emotions and thoughts are not dependent on anyone else's. I had to learn how to become codependent no more! In storms, it's easy to be tossed back and forth in the turmoil or deep muddy waters by others who aren't good for us. As humans, we are deceitful by nature, so if we aren't seeking the Lord, we can steer our loved ones in the wrong direction.

Do you find yourself being tossed back and forth? Are you being blown here and there? Who is your godly counsel? Who is looking to you for godly counsel?

God wants us to speak life and truth in love to those around us hurting. We are to encourage them to seek Jesus. The people God puts in our paths are the ones we need to pay attention to for how we can be used for His glory.

"TO PREPARE GOD'S PEOPLE FOR WORKS OF SERVICE,
SO THAT THE BODY OF CHRIST MAY BE BUILT UP UNTIL
WE ALL REACH UNITY IN THE FAITH AND IN THE
KNOWLEDGE OF THE SON OF GOD AND BECOME MATURE,
ATTAINING TO THE WHOLE MEASURE OF THE FULLNESS
OF CHRIST. THEN WE WILL NO LONGER BE INFANTS,
TOSSED BACK AND FORTH BY THE WAVES, AND BLOWN
HERE AND THERE BY EVERY WIND OF TEACHING AND
BY THE CUNNING AND CRAFTINESS OF MEN IN THEIR
DECEITFUL SCHEMING. INSTEAD, SPEAKING THE TRUTH
IN LOVE, WE WILL IN ALL THINGS GROW UP INTO HIM
WHO IS THE HEAD, THAT IS, CHRIST."

Ephesians 4:12-15

CHAPTER TEN

WORSHIP IN
THE WAVES
carley marcouillier

Can I be honest? Life does not look like I thought it would. At twenty-eight, I still struggle with the silence of so many unanswered prayers. Many of my dreams still seem so distant. Although my life is full, sometimes waves of grief give way to questioning God's plan in this prolonged period of waiting. What do I do with the waves? And how do I fight for faith when pain is still present?

Through my journey, I have identified three specific seasons of my life. I have struggled to navigate the waves of silence and surrender. These unexpected subplots themed by feelings of shame and sadness sought to sabotage my salvation story and, for some time, shattered my sense of security and identity as Christ's child. Yet, it was within the waves of doubt and distortion, I have learned to cling to Christ like never before. The three pain points of my story include my sexuality, my sin, and my singleness.

I find it heartbreaking that sexuality is still considered taboo in the church today because I believe it is one of the most unspoken pains that women carry in our Christian culture. My heart breaks for others who also know the depth of this pain. In battling the brokenness of sexuality, fueled by a backdrop of daddy issues and negative relationship experiences, I fell prey to shame's distortions. Thus, began the internal spiral.

As I drew the attention of women, not men, I questioned everything about myself. I remained silent in my struggle due to the stigma surrounding sexuality. Pain in the form of shame was loudest this season as I wrestled with my faith and feelings. It was here, I learned that shame and silence have a way of supporting sin. This second pain point of my story fed off of the isolation and confusion that began to unravel in my life. My heart became tangled within this season, and I was hit with a wave of pain I will never forget. It was a complex combination of shame and struggle, which I wish ended swiftly.

For the first time in my life, I felt lost because I almost let go of Jesus. I almost walked away from what I knew to be true, allowing sin to steal away the story that Christ had redeemed on the cross. Within the waves of my self-inflicted sin, I walked so far from the girl who loved God. It was here, I pled with God, asking Him to breathe new life into my heart, new truth into my mind, new perspective into my soul. By God's grace, He calmed the storm as I learned what it meant to surrender to the Spirit's power to break strongholds.

But waves still come even years later. Still, I struggle with the unanswered prayers of marriage and motherhood. In the waves of loneliness, it is hard to see God's hand. Some days I feel full, while others feed my longing to be loved. I have battled unbelief, struggling to reconcile that marriage, although beautiful, is not a promise of God.

As I continue to wrestle with want versus worship, I am reminded that my ultimate purpose is to live for the One I serve in whatever season He places me in. In these areas of my story, I have learned that pain comes in various forms but knowing what to do in its wake is vital to finding victory. In looking back to scripture, I have found such comfort in the story and example of Hannah.

Her story of surrender is found in 1 Samuel chapter 1. Hannah's pain was in her inability to have children. The text explains this unmet desire weighed heavily on her to where she could not eat and was completely overwhelmed with grief (1 Samuel 1;7).

But what I find most powerful about Hannah's process in her pain, her grief, and the wave of her waiting, she responds with honest prayer. For the scripture says, "She was deeply distressed and prayed to the Lord and wept bitterly" (I Samuel 1:10).

Hannah's example of worshiping in the waves of pain is such a powerful process. First, she held space for pain (I Samuel 1:10), she pressed into prayer (I Samuel 11-16), and she remained faithful through praise. (I Samuel 1:19)

I love her unrestrained vulnerability and surrender before the Lord! What I learn from Hannah's story and my own is that when pain is present, it is an opportunity to be honest, position myself before the Lord, and continued to praise Him for His faithfulness in my life.

As I follow Hannah's example, I am daily invited to cry out to the Lord praying, petitioning, and praising Him for His goodness and grace. And I am convinced that, like Hannah, God will, in due time, fulfill His plan for me (I Samuel 1:19-20).

DEVOTION
andrea bourgeois

When we find ourselves in storms or rising water due to storms in our life, there will be a time for us to lie bare before the Lord and be exposed for His truth to shine in us once the water resides.

The thick woods near our house that once stood as thick, lush green barriers between us and the neighborhoods, now are cleared and thinned out, with only a few bare broken and weathered trees standing. The tree branches are exposed. It's not lush and green anymore. It may take a few years for the changing seasons to regrow those areas, but they are exposed and bare for all to see for the time being.

Just like rising waters in a storm in the ocean or from the storm surge, the waters will subside, and all that was underwater will be exposed. It might take months for it to fully dry, but it will be revealed.

God will use a storm or season of rising water to expose our struggles so we can call upon Him for help. Sometimes we get so comfortable or tangled with our life we think we don't need Him or want Him. He still wants us, though!

Asking the Lord for help in our struggles and reading His word will help us expose the areas in our life we need to bring forth to His feet and surrender. The Bible is living and active. He will speak to us while we read it. It might take us a while to understand what He's trying to tell us, but if we approach Him with a willing and open heart as we read, then He'll speak to us where we'll hear Him.

Are you worshiping Him in the waves? Do you feel like you or areas in your life have been exposed? Are you seeking His word for guidance? Are you drowning in the high waters and afraid of being exposed when the waters subside?

Our Lord and Savior loves us. He wants us to want His help, and in return, He helps us process life and all our mess.

"For the word of God is living and active, sharper than any double-edged sword, it penetrates even to dividing soul and Spirit, joints and marrow; it judges the thoughts and attitudes of the heart. Nothing in all creation is hidden from God's sight. Everything is uncovered and laid bare before the eyes of Him to whom we must give account."

Hebrews 4: 12-13

CHAPTER ELEVEN

——RESUSCITATE AND——
REVIVE
stefanee tolbert

I was in tenth grade the first time I encountered the presence of God. Don't get me wrong, I knew all about Him. I was raised in the church and was there every single time the doors were opened. My mom was the children's church leader, and the church was an extension of our daily lives.

My first real encounter with God happened when I went through a dark time in high school. It all started with a relationship, as all great high school stories do. What began with me feeling rejected quickly grew into something much more profound. Rejection I had faced as a younger child resurfaced, and I was much too young to understand my emotions and how to deal with them. Depression took over.

I had gotten to a place of such dark depression. I would wear the same Gap hoodie every day, I didn't shower (I'm sure that hoodie smelled great), I didn't care about school, my grades suffered, I even switched schools for a semester. I had allowed the lies of the enemy to make me feel worthless. What started as something so small had grown in my mind into something that was no longer about any one thing. It was about my identity. When depression takes over, all rational thinking goes out of the window.

The enemy is real, and depression is real. Suicide is at an all-time high, so please don't discredit anyone whom you are worried about.

After a while, my body reacted to how I was treating it, and I got sick and fragile for six months. One rainy afternoon I went into my backyard. I was ill, weak, depressed, and I didn't even know what I was depressed about. I just was. It wasn't one thing; it was my entire life. I was just tired of living it.

My dad was working on the guest house and had left his tools outside. I sat in the backyard, in the pouring rain, thinking about which tool I could use to take my life. Next to his toolbox was a pair of hedge trimmers. I picked them up and rocked back and forth as I sat on the ground crying, out of control.

At that moment, I cried out to God from a place of desperation—real desperation. I begged Him to show up. I yelled out to Him, "Where are you? Are you even real? Do you even care?" I remember closing my eyes, still rocking back and forth, and a slideshow played in my mind. I remember it so vividly. Pictures of my childhood; pictures of things I had gone through in my life; times I had cried myself to sleep after my grandmother, whom I loved more than anything, had passed away; times when I was broken, hurting, scared, rejected, or sad. Some of the most incredible times in my life were projected in my mind. I saw moments of absolute brokenness and moments of pure joy. It was a slideshow of my life, and every picture had two things in common: I was there, and Jesus was there.

This warmth came over me, and, at that moment, I knew Jesus loved me, I knew He cared about the details, and I knew He was there. It was the first time in my life I experienced His presence. No one could ever convince me that God wasn't real or that He didn't care. He met me in the pouring rain. This broken teenager whom He gave His life for. I cried out, and my amazing heavenly Father wrapped His loving arms around me in an almost tangible way.

At that moment, I gave my life to God. I knew that He was real. I had grown up knowing about Him. I knew the surface-level things. I had learned the books of the Bible at four years old, but at that moment, I went from knowing of Him to knowing Him. This moment in time changed the trajectory of my life forever.

My story of salvation is a beautiful story, although walking through it was anything but beautiful. As the co-founder and principal of a school, I work with children every day. My absolute passion is working with teenagers.

I now know that God allowed me to walk through that tough season so I could one day see a greasy-haired teen wearing a hoodie (as most teenagers do, no matter how hot it is outside), looking like the weight of the world is on their shoulders, and see them for who they are inside and who they will be. I can talk to them and help them see there is so much purpose on the other side of their pain. I explain to them I understand what they are going through, and, in those moments, they open.

I have had the incredible opportunity to lead countless youth to a relationship with Him. I now host retreats for teens, and I cannot tell you the number of times I have shared my experience of finding Jesus, which resonated with a teen. Through sharing this piece of my story, I have been able to pull so many young people out of some very dark seasons. In my life, I have story after story of times when I walked through a dark season, and from it came something so beautiful.

We can stand in every season and every hard place knowing He works all things for the good of those who love Him and who are called according to His purpose. He is faithful to His Word, and He makes beauty from ashes.

NOTHING IS EVER WASTED.

DEVOTION
andrea bourgeois

According to Merriam-Webster Dictionary...

resuscitate: to revive from apparent death or from unconsciousness

revive: to return to consciousness or life: become active or flourishing again.

Until we encounter God's love in a personal way, we just know about Him and His love. Some will go a lifetime without experiencing our Heavenly Father that they've read about their whole life.

Life is like a storm. It dies down at times and can be peaceful, while at other times it can be tumultuous and full of disorder. To overcome our overwhelming obstacles, we must ask God to resuscitate or revive us according to His will and His way. No matter how far into a disaster we find ourselves in or how deep into raging waters we end up in, God can save us. No matter how dark our world may seem, God can see us and reach us.

"I WILL BE GLAD AND REJOICE IN YOUR LOVE,
FOR YOU SAW MY AFFLICTION
AND KNEW THE ANGUISH OF MY SOUL.
YOU HAVE NOT GIVEN ME INTO THE HANDS OF THE ENEMY
BUT HAVE SET MY FEET IN A SPACIOUS PLACE.

BE MERCIFUL TO ME, LORD, FOR I AM IN DISTRESS.

MY EYES GROW WEAK WITH SORROW,
MY SOUL AND BODY WITH GRIEF.
MY LIFE IS CONSUMED BY ANGUISH
AND MY YEARS BY GROANING.
MY STRENGTH FAILS BECAUSE OF MY AFFLICTION,
AND MY BONES GROW WEAK.

BECAUSE OF ALL MY ENEMIES,
I AM THE UTTER CONTEMPT OF MY NEIGHBORS
AND AN OBJECT OF DREAD TO MY CLOSEST FRIENDS—
THOSE WHO SEE ME ON THE STREET FLEE FROM ME.

I AM FORGOTTEN AS THOUGH I WERE DEAD.
I HAVE BECOME LIKE BROKEN POTTERY."

Psalm 31:7-12

CHAPTER TWELVE

IN THE
NIGHT
gabbi hartzell

I grew up in a single-parent household most of my life. From the age of three, it was just my mom, sister, and me — a house full of girls. My dad loved Jesus and his family but loved a strong drink and drugs a bit more. He had been abusive towards my mother for years, and after a long time of fighting and striving, she made the courageous choice to protect her daughters and kick him out.

Perhaps this had something to do with my decision to follow Jesus. In second grade, I sat in school and read a story about a boy who followed Jesus and had joy, something I wanted more of, even at seven. At that moment, I sat quietly and asked Jesus into my life. That is when my relationship with Him began. Still, it would be twenty-one years later when that relationship would be tested beyond imagination.

When I was twenty-eight years old, my best friend found out she had cervical cancer while pregnant with her second child. She was my rock, my most generous supporter and encourager, fiercely loyal, and the one and only person who knew everything about me. When we found out, it rocked our worlds. She, too, made a tough choice, putting her child's needs first and deciding to put off harsher treatments until after he was born to preserve his life. Once he arrived, she fought hard for four months until she could resist no longer.

I spent days in the hospital with her but had to return home one night for an event my ministry was holding. At 4 a.m., I got a call from her sister telling me that my dearest friend had breathed her last breath. It felt like the breath had also been knocked out of me. I immediately got in the car and drove an hour to the hospital, begging and pleading with Jesus the whole way there to save my friend. To bring her back to life the way He did His friend, Lazarus...

HE DID NOT.

I was still praying and making my request for Him to breathe life back into her body...

HE DID NOT.

At first, this devastation caused me to want to live my life with more vigor, more purpose, more passion than ever before. Instead of dealing with my loss, I kept moving until it dealt with me. I started falling into a major depression when I got hit with another loss — my father. Those relationships were vastly different, but grief is grief. And it was more than I could handle.

I began spiraling out of control — while putting on a brave face and continuing to lead a ministry. Still, behind closed doors, I was falling apart. After a while, I no longer recognized myself. I began pushing my friends away, my husband away, and even God away. In those months, I did more screaming at Him than talking to Him. I couldn't understand why He would do this to me after all I had done for Him and told Him I wanted nothing to do with Him. As I led worship on Sundays, my praise was a pretense, and I refused to sing [audibly] the words "You are good." To me, He was not.

When forced to lead a group of women through a book on prayer,

I knew I had to say some words we were asked to pray despite my anger towards Him. So, I did. After a few months of repeating the empty words, "I want You to be the driving desire of my life," the Holy Spirit began working on me without me even knowing. He began answering the words I was heartlessly muttering.

When He softened my heart just enough for me to be open, He introduced me to a woman who lived out the words I had been uttering. I saw a desire in her for Jesus that I had never seen before. I saw a delight in her that sprang from knowing Him deeply. And I recognized within her the same thing that I had longed for years prior when I was seven and sitting at that school desk in second grade. Here He was again, knocking on the door of my heart, holding in His hand what I had been missing and desperately looking for — joy. After so many months of darkness, I was craving it. So, I went home that evening, sat down with an open Bible, open journal, open mind, and said five simple words, "Okay, God. Let's do this." From that moment on, everything changed.

He cultivated within me a real and deep yearning for Him. He began developing within me a desire to know Him. He used the previous darkness in my life to help light the path for others. And He showed me that though there had been so many moments of mourning I had experienced, genuine joy was possible, attainable, and anchored in Him.

I could again sing the words—you are good—because I found my circumstances do not define my God. I could point others in life's tragedies to Him because He truly is our Rock and firm foundation. I could show people how desiring Him really is possible because all you must do is simply ask Him for it.

Through all the anger, all the hurt, all the darkness — when I had turned my back on Him, He never turned His back on me. Even when I tried so incredibly hard to let go of Him, He never let go of me. I found that though "sorrow may last for the night," joy indeed does come in the morning when we turn to Him.

DEVOTION
andrea bourgeois

Some storms strengthen at night because the upper and middle part of the atmosphere cools, and energy is released in the storms causing more winds and rain. Rita hit my hometown at 2:38 a.m. on September 24, 2005, and Laura made landfall shortly after midnight on August 27, 2020.

I hurt the most at night when I'm in the middle of a trial or storm. In the night is where the enemy tries to tempt me, and it's when my mind goes down a rabbit hole of the "what if's" or the "woe's me" pity party. It's in the night that we lay in bed with our thoughts racing and our hearts bursting.

A hurricane or a tornado will never be as powerful as our Lord God! That almost seems impossible to conceive and comprehend those thoughts. I stand amid the aftermath, and our God is more powerful than this! And our God's power is for our good and for our help, not destruction. His love for us is so vast.

HE LOVES LIKE A HURRICANE!

"WEEPING MAY REMAIN FOR A NIGHT BUT REJOICING COMES IN THE MORNING."

The scripture and saying, "THIS TOO SHALL PASS," is so true after a storm. God is with us through the whole thing, and it doesn't last forever. We will sing and smile again.

Are you able to see God's power and love for you? Do you weep in the night silently? I'm right there with you! Hang in there with me because joy is coming in the morning.

"THE VOICE OF THE LORD IS OVER THE WATERS, THE GOD OF GLORY THUNDERS, THE LORD THUNDERS OVER THE MIGHTY WATERS. THE VOICE OF THE LORD IS POWERFUL; THE VOICE OF THE LORD IS MAJESTIC."

"THE VOICE OF THE LORD STRIKES WITH FLASHES OF LIGHTNING."

"THE VOICE OF THE LORD TWISTS THE OAKS AND STRIPS THE FORESTS BARE. AND IN HIS TEMPLE ALL CRY, "GLORY!""

"WEEPING MAY REMAIN FOR A NIGHT BUT REJOICING COMES IN THE MORNING."

"THIS TOO SHALL PASS,"

Psalm 29:3-4, 7, 9 and Psalm 30:5

CHAPTER THIRTEEN

INNER
CYCLONE
rachael adams

"If you could see yourself through my eyes it would change your world," my husband lovingly encouraged me when we were first married. Bless his heart then and now for having to give me a never-ending pep talk in an effort to build my confidence.

He confessed recently that when he first met me he felt like I was just fishing for a compliment, but as he began to get to know me he realized I really did doubt my value and worth.

For as long as I remember I have battled insecurity. My husband, parents, and friends can give me words of affirmation and validation until they are blue in the face, but their words have never taken residence in my heart.

Even as a Christian woman who knows my identity in Christ, I still find it difficult to feel like it and live like it on a daily basis. I know I am fearfully and wonderfully made in God's image. I know I am chosen, loved, and redeemed. And yet it's difficult to consistently live out these truths.

All my life I've wanted so badly to feel like enough, but have never felt like I am enough. Not smart enough, talented enough, thin enough, pretty enough, kind enough, successful enough — the list could go on. Maybe you can relate?

Today's image-saturated society has exacerbated the problem. We are face-to-face with unrealistic standards that cause us to feel even more inadequate. There is always something more or better and if we ever get "there," then the mark just keeps moving. So we strive, work harder, and do more to try to prove that we aren't inadequate after all.

But the thing is, we don't want to just be adequate. We want to be perfect. Even as I type that sentence, I know perfection on earth does not exist. Only Jesus was perfect. So why are we striving for something unattainable?

This cycle of feeling inadequate, then performing to prove our adequacy is exhausting and will surely end in defeat. I'm left to wonder then, why are we staying on this cycle? The only answer I can surmise is fear. I'm afraid of messing up, being rejected, disliked, and failing. I'm afraid of how others will view me.

So the question is, how do we move past our fear? Scripture tells us perfect love casts out fear (1 John 4:18). God's perfection, not mine or yours. I hope this frees your heart like it does mine. Because sister, you and I actually don't have what it takes. Not in and of ourselves. We feel inadequate because we are inadequate. We can not fulfill the law perfectly, we are not sufficient, we are weak, and we do lack on our own.

The good news is that God's power is made perfect in weakness (2 Corinthians 12:9) Thank goodness because that's how I feel most days. He knew we were weak and couldn't live this life on our own, so He came to save us and leave us the Holy Spirit to enable and empower us.

In fact, He says when we are weak, then we are strong (2 Corinthians 12:10). He is simply asking us to be willing to offer all we are and all we have to Him in faith and believe it is enough.

BELIEVE.

These fears, doubts, insecurities, and unworthiness are all really a form of disbelief. It wasn't just faith in myself I was lacking, it was a lack of faith in Him. Regrettably, I'd put my hope and faith in me, rather than in the One who created me.

To counteract this line of thinking, I've begun to pray, "Lord I believe, help my unbelief (Mark 9:24)." The Holy Spirit will help lead, guide, direct, convict, and strengthen me to do whatever He has called me to do. And the same is true for you. We have ALL we need for life and godliness (2 Peter 1:3) because He has given us ALL of Him.

When we really believe this, our confidence comes not in what we are offering of ourselves then, but rather because we are offering Him. If you are feeling inadequate and insecure like me, I pray you see yourself through the clear lens of the Word of God and not the skewed lens of the world. It's time to take God at His Word and believe it with our head and our heart.

Just like my husband encouraged me, God wants to encourage and equip you with a never-ending pep talk filled with His never-ending love. Do you hear Him whispering to your heart today? If only you could see yourself through My eyes, it would change your world.

But here's the thing, God doesn't just want it to change our world, He wants us to take what He's given us to introduce others to Him, so He can change their world too.

DEVOTION
andrea bourgeois

The Bible says in John 16 that in this world we will have trouble, but to take heart because Jesus overcame the world. We find ourselves in all different storms in life, varying from massive ones with destruction like a hurricane visible on the outside of every home and building. But we also experience smaller storms that only affect remote areas, and sometimes those aren't visible to the eye. These storms overtime can create destruction if left unchecked or unnoticed.

The storm in our mind can create a swirling cyclone that leads us down a negative spiral leaving us to feel helpless and hopeless. Whether you find yourself struggling with self-worth, overcoming perfectionism, enduring mental illness, or rebuking negative thought patterns, God is right there with you. He wants us to look to Him for guidance on changing our thought patterns and responses to life with His help!

God allows all the different variations of strengths and types of storms in our lives. He sees how what may have been meant for our misery can be used for His glory. Do you find yourself in an emotional or mental storm where you feel trapped and isolated? Are you your own worst critic and the author of your own storm? Have you been through trauma that has caused your mind to replay the events on repeat? Or are you in the downward self-perpetuating cycle of negativity and low self-esteem spiraling down and close to making landfall?

Take a moment and acknowledge the pain you are experiencing is real. You alone cannot overcome it. Jesus wants to renew your mind. He wants to reroute your thoughts and help pull you out of your spiraling cyclone onto safe ground. Then once you are safe, you will see His perfect and pleasing will for your life!

"DO NOT CONFORM ANY LONGER TO THE PATTERN OF THIS WORLD BUT BE TRANSFORMED BY THE RENEWING OF YOUR MIND. THEN YOU WILL BE ABLE TO TEST AND APPROVE WHAT GOD'S WILL IS - HIS GOOD, PLEASING AND PERFECT WILL."

Romans 12:2

CHAPTER FOURTEEN

EXPOSED TO
LIGHT
becky beresford

I never wanted to have a broken marriage. Like many little girls, Disney brainwashed me to believe marriages would end in "happily ever after's" and golden sunsets. Turns out, making two people into one is a messy venture, and it often comes with unexpected heartache. But God is in the miracle-making business, and He loves to show His faithfulness by bringing the dead back to life.

I met my husband, Madison, at a summer camp in Ohio. We were both counselors, helping kids come to know Jesus on the shores of Lake Erie. My thirteen-year-old brother was assigned as Madison's camper. I can still remember him awkwardly saying, "Madison has the hots for you." At first, I was shocked my little brother knew what the 'hots' was. Deeper down, I didn't believe him.

But as Madison pursued me, God shifted my heart toward him. I was drawn to his passion for healing others and bringing them into the Kingdom. I also learned he came from a broken family. Trauma marked his past, with neglect, emotional manipulation, and abuse making regular appearances. His parents were newly divorced, and he told me dating would be hard on him (and probably me). His heart was like a rubber band—stretching when trying to love me, then bouncing back into the protective posture he used for survival.

I was good with it at first. I saw myself as an instrument of God's kindness and grace. But soon, arguments developed between us, and my baggage was laid bare. Fear, shame, and anxiety followed me ever since I was young. The people-pleaser in me was strong because I learned good girls get good things, particularly love and acceptance. I took the enemy's bait and believed I needed to earn my worth. I would sacrifice myself at all costs to make others happy, but inside I resented it. By the time we got married, my husband and I went through multiple toxic cycles, feeding off one another's wounded places. We promised we would never fight like our parents. And we didn't. We fought worse.

God has given power to the tongue—it speaks life or death. When Madison and I were doing good, we were doing great! But when we fought, we let the enemy have full control. I said things to him I never thought I'd ever say to anyone! Words that poured out of our mouths were fatal. Emotional abuse was something we both experienced and rendered. Conflict patterns we wanted to break free from seemed like they would never end. We went to multiple counselors. We did our homework. Madison even studied to be a counselor and opened his own practice. I worked in women's ministry and wrote encouragement for women. Meanwhile, my own heart was breaking.

I kept thinking about the summer we met—two people who loved Jesus and wanted to serve Him. Now we were so angry with each other. Our relationship continued to spiral, affecting our children and landing at rock bottom in 2019. I was done. And I let him know it.

While looking up costs for divorce, the Holy Spirit whispered to my heart and told me to trust Him. I had been praying for our marriage for ten years. For a decade, I was striving, waiting, believing God would come through for us. But now I felt depressed. I had anxiety attacks to the point of not being able to write or speak. Madison's body was shutting down where he couldn't walk. Suicidal thoughts surfaced. Our outlook appeared hopeless.

SO, I GOT FRANK WITH GOD.

"Lord, where are You? Do You hear our cries or care? You say You want our marriage restored, but I doubt You'll answer. I'm done, but You tell me You are not. Well, I can't do this anymore... I surrender... This battle is Yours."

It was December, but earlier that year, God gave me a word for the year. MIRACLE. Madison was going to South Carolina for a work Christmas party. Before leaving, he saw videos from a Christian organization where people were experiencing freedom from emotional pain and were healed. They were having a conference at the same time he would be in South Carolina. The Holy Spirit nudged him to have someone pray with him. Desperate to meet God and experience relief, Madison grabbed a taxi after work and headed to the event. He didn't know a soul and was sitting alone when a man approached him. He asked Madison about his walk with God and then asked if any part of his body hurt. Madison told him his neck was hurting, so the guy put his hand on him and prayed, but this was no ordinary prayer.

Immediately he prayed off different bondage Madison had been wrestling with for years. He never met this guy, but it was like he was reading a checklist of his dirty laundry, casting off things he had never told others.

In a matter of minutes, the Holy Spirit delivered my husband from decades of trauma, abuse, depression, and abandonment. Madison said it was like twenty wool sweaters were ripped off his chest, and he could breathe in the love of Jesus for the first time. That night, God answered my prayers and did the miraculous. My husband became a different man.

God changed our lives in a moment and made the impossible... possible. He set that meeting up. He knew what He was doing. He brought about His purpose in His perfect time.

My husband's transformation ushered in more profound healing in my soul. Jesus showed me I am worthy of His blessings (including answered prayers!), not because I earn them but because I am His. He brought areas of my life into the light where I needed to repent and walked me into a new level of freedom in His love.

The old was gone. A new day for our marriage has come. And it's far better than any surface-level fairytale. It's the deep work of a Creator who heals our heartache and promises to redeem every tear.

DEVOTION
andrea bourgeois

Our deep secrets and things we struggle with are often hidden and buried so deep that God's light can't shine through to reach it. God allows storm winds like a hurricane to come in a sweep over the trees and vegetation to defoliate the canopies for sunlight to reach the soil of once dark, damp ground. Our secrets and sinful areas can create traps or soggy areas where we are more suspectable to keep hidden and to get stuck without a way out by our means. Our Father loves us and sees our pain. He will allow the winds to come in and tear down whatever walls necessary to expose the damp, soggy ground in our lives.

What areas in your life do you have hidden and need God to expose some sunlight? Are you looking at your life as a checklist and making sure you cross all the t's and dot all the i's instead of revealing and surrendering all areas to God for true meaningful worship? Are the winds of a storm bending you to your breaking point? Are there walls that need to come down? What are your hidden dark, damp, and soggy areas in your life?

God will expose the darkness in our life. He will help us shine His love and light in those areas for us to continue to grow in Him. Reflect what He's done in our life to those around us.

"THIS IS THE MESSAGE WE HAVE HEARD FROM HIM AND DECLARE TO YOU: GOD IS LIGHT; IN HIM, THERE IS NO DARKNESS AT ALL. IF WE CLAIM TO HAVE FELLOWSHIP WITH HIM YET WALK IN THE DARKNESS, WE LIE AND DO NOT LIVE BY THE TRUTH. BUT IF WE WALK IN THE LIGHT, AS HE IS IN THE LIGHT, WE HAVE FELLOWSHIP WITH ONE ANOTHER, AND THE BLOOD OF JESUS, HIS SON, PURIFIES US FROM ALL SIN."

1 John 1: 5–7

CHAPTER FIFTEEN

STRIPPED TO
EQUIPPED
megan ethridge

Rock bottom, have you ever been there? Kicked in the gut, gasping for air, hanging on by a thread; frantically searching for something to grab hold of with what feels like wearing blackout glasses. It's a lonely, agonizing, often necessary place to be. My rock bottom was what I had ALWAYS pictured as the epitome of love, joy, and happiness.

I've been babysitting since the age of twelve. When I discovered we were pregnant, I knew it would be different because this baby was my flesh and blood, but I also thought, *I got this. I've been taking care of kids for twenty years.* Woah, I was SO not prepared for postpartum depression coupled with a child injured along the way--stuck in fight or flight mode. What does that mean? Well, for one, WE. NEVER. SLEPT. I'm not talking about a baby who wakes up to nurse and falls back asleep while nursing. He never slept more than one to two hours at a time, his naps were twenty to thirty minutes long, and he frequently woke at 3-3:30 a.m. FOR. THE. DAY.

He needed to be held constantly, was filled with severe anxiety, and would never allow me to put him down and walk out of the room for even two minutes. I was exhausted, depleted, and emotionally drained!

Are there better/bolder words than those?! because if so, that's what I was. I spiraled into postpartum depression-fighting to keep my head above water, all the while inhaling liters a day. I was in a dark place, nearly drowning, and clawing at everything trying not to go under. I became SO ANGRY and was filled with a rage I had never experienced before. People love to ask, "How's motherhood? Don't you love it?!" While I gave some truth to our situation, I usually flashed a fake smile and said, "It's the best." Although, what I was living, I hated.

The one thing I knew intuitively and can now whole-heartedly say was all from the Lord was this statement, "The medicine you practice will not heal him." I am a registered nurse, who at this time, had ten years of experience with all of them working in the critical care setting. My mothering instinct and that statement sent me on a fierce search of the medicine that would. During this journey, I wondered if my struggling health, especially postpartum depression, affected my son's health. At different points on our journey, I would occasionally inquire about this to the practitioner we were seeing. Some put it off, assuring me it wasn't related. Others acknowledged it was a possibility, but that X step needed to be taken first, and how my health affected him could be addressed later.

Finally, our last practitioner (who we still see and is a huge mentor in my life) not only validated my thoughts, but simultaneously treated and taught me just how impactful my health was to my son and husband's health.

Looking back, that was rock bottom for me; however, it's not as painful to reminisce about when viewing it with another lens. The lens of perspective. That God needed me there (that hard, awful place) to learn how vital overall health is. He also needed me there to unearth a purpose He had planned for me. That purpose is to teach other moms how important our physical, mental, emotional, and spiritual states affect our mind/body/soul; these states directly affect our husbands and children's health and well-being. Was that season pretty?! Heck no, the craziest, ugliest version of me to date, just ask my husband and close family. Did

I make it harder than it had to be? Absolutely, I had a mediocre prayer life with little self-awareness of myself or my health and a poor ability to examine my own needs. Was it necessary? A million times, a resounding Y-E-S!! Rock bottom is where I had to be to understand that He created me to be the best version of myself. That best version included all of me: mental, physical, spiritual, and emotional.

I'd love to tell you I saw God's hand in it all during that hard, dark place; however, that's not my story. Several years into my motherhood journey, I felt Him calling me out of the mediocre and into a deeper relationship with Him. (Fun fact; I started that deeper relationship with Andrea's Bible Study, Just Breathe!!) As I dove in, He taught me to trust His faithfulness and omnipresence with me in ALL THINGS. He also revealed that He was not only with me during my darkest time, but in it, He had a purpose for my pain:

HEAL MOTHERS. HEAL FAMILIES. HEAL THE WORLD.

It's only through Him, with Him, and in Him, I can share my story and spread His message of health and hope.

DEVOTION
andrea bourgeois

We may never understand why God allows the storms to swoop in until years after when true healing and restoration begin. - Sometimes we can't see the why when we are in it!

Why does God allow snowstorms, tornadoes, hurricanes, wildfires, tsunamis, earthquakes, or any other natural disaster or storm to come and demolish whatever is in its path? Why does He allow the storms in our life to come in and wreak havoc in our lives?

If you're like me, I catch myself angry with God when I plead with Him and ask, "WHY? Why did you allow this to happen to me? WHY!?"

Sometimes we'll never know why storms come literally or figuratively in our path. Sometimes when we are in it, we know God will use our pain somehow and someway. And sometimes, it isn't until way after our storm has passed that we see His hand in our lives, and we see His purpose.

Each storm or trial we face, God is molding us and refining us with fire to become the purest form we can become through Himself. Our goal isn't an earthly focus but a heavenly one.

You may see those who have weathered storm after storm and radiate a beaming joy from within them. That joy isn't from this earthly place. It's from our heavenly destination.

God will strip us down only to equip us fully for His purpose to be revealed.

Have you found yourself in a trial for some time now? Do you see that God is pruning you in the process? Ask God to fill you with His promise in 1Peter 1 of an inexpressible and glorious joy in your sorrow and sadness that surrounds you.

God wants to heal our families and us. He wants to heal our nation and our world. These storms are just part of it!

"IN THIS, YOU GREATLY REJOICE, THOUGH NOW FOR
A LITTLE WHILE YOU MAY HAVE HAD TO SUFFER GRIEF
IN ALL KINDS OF TRIALS. THESE HAVE COME SO THAT
YOUR FAITH – OF GREATER WORTH THAN GOLD, WHICH
PERISHES EVEN THOUGH REMINDED BY FIRE – MAY BE
PROVED GENUINE AND MAY RESULT IN PRAISE,
GLORY, AND HONOR WHEN JESUS CHRIST IS REVEALED.
THOUGH YOU HAVE NOT SEEN HIM, YOU LOVE HIM; AND
EVEN THOUGH YOU DO NOT SEE HIM NOW, YOU BELIEVE
IN HIM AND ARE FILLED WITH AN INEXPRESSIBLE AND
GLORIOUS JOY, FOR YOU ARE RECEIVING THE GOAL OF
YOUR FAITH, THE SALVATION OF YOUR SOULS."

1 Peter 1:6-9

CHAPTER SIXTEEN

——— RESCUED ———
natalie miller

> **"IF YOU FIND IN YOURSELF A DESIRE IN WHICH
> NOTHING IN THIS WORLD CAN SATISFY, THE
> OBVIOUS EXPLANATION IS YOU WERE MADE FOR
> ANOTHER WORLD."**
>
> *CS Lewis*

I kept looking. I searched knowing my efforts would pay off. And they did, eventually, just not in the way I hoped. In those years, I looked behind me and saw a wake of broken and abusive relationships, a lost child, parents dying from cancer, and a girl trying to find her way into the world. And looking forward I saw nothing on the horizon. Nothing was bright or shiny or noteworthy, and that was the scariest part- the nothingness, the constant lack of vision for the future.

When it crumbled I shifted from wanting to walk this worn path to wanting a brand new path. I was tired of being tired. I was tired of trying to find love from people and places in moments and experiences. I was tired of trying to feel secure in what I did. I was tired of hurting people I loved and hurting myself in little ways.

Step by step I walked away from my oldness and into a newness. The process seemed elusive and uncharted, but I felt clean and new for the first time in a long time. I was at peace in a season of life with the full fury of a storm. The new choices felt right. I couldn't deny that the old way was uncomfortable and sometimes unbearable.

That's where Jesus met me; in all my sin. He called me out of darkness and into His glorious light. He called me while in the lowest valley and in the darkest time. He rescued me from myself and rearranged what I could not manage any longer. I fell into His ways and relished being loved by a man I had only talked about but never "known." He became my best friend when I had none. Jesus walked me through the lowest time in my life, and I leaned on Him like He was breath and life itself. And it changed me. It changed everything about me.

Jesus set me apart. He pulled me out of the mire and set me on solid ground. This process wasn't easy. It was work every day. The Bible says not to be conformed by the world but to be transformed by the renewing of our mind. Renewing our minds brings healing and wholeness to our innermost being. It's not just a good work, it's a necessary one.

This season came with a process I will call Mapping Out Life. I circled around the events that had stuck out or plagued me all these years after knowing Christ. One by one I would sit with Jesus and bring up these different circumstances and ask for Him to show me His truth about it. The more I sought Him out, the more Jesus drew me in. This became a long season of my life, and I felt a need to walk the road with Him through those valleys I never wanted to revisit. But with Him, I would. He would meet me in these moments of worship and prayer when I asked Him for wisdom and showed me a new name and a new side to the sad story I had rehearsed all those years. The process and new perspective changed me.

It was healing to revisit these past events and see His perspective. He would always show me He was there and give me sweet words to hold onto or scriptures to rehearse that forever changed my life for His glory. Spending time with Jesus in His Word or on my knees in worship brought me to new places in Him. It's as if He would elevate my spirit when I would spend this sacred time with Him. It was worth it! I held my head higher, I laughed louder, and day by day I understood more that I was not only saved but set FREE!

DEVOTION
andrea bourgeois

Hurricane Harvey hit our neighboring cities to the west of us a few years before Hurricane Laura. I downloaded the Zello app and listened as residents were frantically radioing in for help on their rooftops because the storm had stalled out and dumped days of rain that led to flooding. The Cajun Navy was formed after Hurricane Katrina in 2005. It's a group of volunteers who come to the rescue of flood victims in times of crisis, and aid in efforts of first responders throughout the Gulf Coast states. With the Zello app, dispatchers and volunteers helped locate the victims. Some of my friends with boats joined in on the cause, and I listened through the app. I prayed all night for the families and small children to be rescued. One of my best friends called me in hysteria as she explained her parents' home was flooding and they couldn't get out. She asked me if I knew anyone with a boat to get them. My heart broke for her and immediately contacted one of my friends who was assisting in the rescue mission. His wife relayed the information to him and he would try his best to find them and get them out of the rising waters. Prayers were answered and they were rescued from another boat.

God is our rescue in all the storms we will encounter. He sees us trapped with rising water and reaches out His hand for us to grab.

God is with us in our trouble, He will deliver us, and He will show and teach us of His ways because He loves us that much.

Are you in the grim or the valley? Do you find yourself trapped with no way out? Are you needing to be rescued by our Lord Jesus?

REACH UP AND ASK HIM FOR HELP! HE WILL!

"Because he loves me," says the Lord, "I will rescue him; I will protect him, for he acknowledges my name. He will call upon me, and I will answer him; I will be with him in trouble, I will deliver him and honor him. With long life will I satisfy him and show him my salvation."

Psalm 91:14-16

CHAPTER SEVENTEEN

ROADBLOCKS
season bowers

I'm an only child, raised in a conservative Christian home and have always loved Jesus. My mom was passionate about educating me on the "sin of premarital sex" and how "abortion was murder." It worked...for a while. As a teen, I was legitimately terrified of sex. I was convinced that not only would God strike me down by lightning, my mother would instinctually know of my sin and kill me. A double murder sending me straight to hell.

At twenty-five, in a committed relationship heading towards marriage I found myself pregnant. I wasn't using birth control but still shocked it happened to me. A naive, invincible twenty something, I couldn't believe what was happening.

One would think that based on my love of Jesus, my conservative Christian upbringing, and committed relationship that I would have told my family and given my mother what she always wanted—a grandbaby.

I. Was. Terrified.

In my home there was a lot of unintentional projected shame and villanization toward, not only premarital sex, but unwed mothers. I was convinced I would be disowned.

That's not true but it seemed easier to keep the truth hidden deep beneath fear.

I contacted a close friend who I knew had multiple abortions. She was not a Christian and aside from my boyfriend, she was the only one I told. She assured me the experience was easy, cheap, and no big deal. In the fog of fear and selfishness, it seemed like the best way to handle "the problem." My boyfriend agreed.

I rationalized it thinking: It's so early, it's not even a "thing" yet. My insurance will pay for it, so it's virtually free. We're going to get married and have kids someday and that will make up for it. I have friends who've done it, and they're fine!

SURELY, GOD WILL FORGIVE ME.

My friend was right. It was quick, practically painless, and only $250 (which my boyfriend paid for). I was in and out within an hour, and we were back at his place to binge watch movies for the day. No one knew, and I would keep it that way.

A year later my mom died. One of my first thoughts was, "Well, she knows now."

I found solace in the fact that the grandbaby my mother so desperately wanted was waiting for her in heaven. Strange that I couldn't acknowledge I was pregnant with an actual baby, but I could imagine her grandchild in heaven.

Eventually all my rationale failed. My marriage didn't last long, I never had children of my own, and my secret clamored inside me.

Technically, I knew I was forgiven. I had repented countless times and had faith in the grace of God to cover my sins. However, I hadn't released the shame and pain. It was easier to pretend it didn't exist, so I told no one and NEVER used the A-word.

Over the next few years, I embarked on a healing journey to address other pain in my life. I was healed from the pain of my divorce and the death of my mother. I understood my worth and value as a daughter of the King. My life was changing dramatically for the better and all the while the Lord kept gently inviting me to "deal with the A-word."

I became a pastor and was heavily involved in a prayer and healing ministry. I saw the Lord mightily free people from bondage and knew it was time. I gathered trusted friends to walk me through an emotional healing prayer session. Having led hundreds of them, I knew what to expect. The person being prayed for asks the Holy Spirit to highlight a memory that the Lord wants to heal, not to cause harm or to re-traumatize, but to reveal God's goodness, presence, and love. The results are powerful.

I was nervous. I had convinced myself that while I was forgiven, what I did was just about the worst thing one could do; the Lord wouldn't show up during that.

Pushing through fear, I asked the Lord to take me to a moment before, during, or after my abortion. I expected to see a picture of me sitting in the waiting room, or in the car on the way home. Nope. Immediately, I saw myself in the procedure, and, to my surprise, Jesus was there! He revealed Himself standing right next to me, holding my hand! But it didn't stop there. He brought my mother with Him.

You may be wondering, "How is that possible?" God is outside of our timeline. He's able to take us back in our mind to reveal the spiritual reality of any situation. In this case, my mother was alive that day with no idea of what was happening. But God in all his grace and mercy brought her with Him to show me how loved I really am.

THAT MOMENT EVERY CHAIN SHATTERED.

The two people who love me the most in all the universe were loving and holding me right where I was. They weren't celebrating what was happening, but they were there with love and compassion. There was no shame, anger, or condemnation - just love. Everything changes when King Jesus shows up. Shame is eclipsed when the glory of God shines. I am not proud of my decision and I do not celebrate my choice. I do, however, celebrate the healing and love available for all people because of the total and complete forgiveness of Jesus Christ. When forgiven, it's not done with a cold shoulder. We are forgiven, loved, hugged, blessed, and restored to an intimate and loving relationship with our good Father in heaven. I have no shame about having had an abortion because Jesus took it all away.

season bowers

DEVOTION
andrea bourgeois

We all have pride in some way or another. It can hinder what God wants to do in our lives, and in our family's lives, especially when we're in a storm in life. When our home was damaged and our yard destroyed from Hurricane Laura, pride kept me from wanting to ask for help. What will other's think of me? But God didn't let pride stand in His way because He sent living hands and feet of the body to help us without asking for it. I remember weeping on our porch out of desperation. Looking back, God was pulling out my pride and replacing it with His love and blessings. Shortly after that meltdown or breakdown, blessings poured out onto us.

In storms, regardless of how you got there, our pride can keep us silent and can rob us of the blessings that God wants to give us. Pride can keep us afraid to speak of the past because we feel safer without going there.

Leviathan, the spirit of pride, is the only spirit given a name in the Bible. The others, like the spirit of addiction or the spirit of poverty, aren't named in the Word. But pride is.

Our enemy temps us, and we fall into the trap of temptation of allowing the spirit of pride to take up residents in our hearts. Pride leeches and carries over into other areas of lives with little or no effort. It's one of the hardest strongholds to break. It's what keeps us deaf to the Word of God and keeps us trapped in shame and guilt. It's a roadblock.

But in Psalm 74, we are told that our God of the universe is the one who crushed the heads of Leviathan. God opens the springs or dries them up. He established the sun and the moon and set all the boundaries of the earth, making summer and winter. God allows the storms to form, and He allows them to make landfall wherever He sees fit.

He has a reason for everything and purpose for it all under His mighty hand.

Are you trying to overcome an area or a circumstance that may be blocked due to pride? Is God revealing to you areas in your life He wants to heal in return for peace and healing? Seek the Lord in your storm and ask Him to reveal to you where He was in your mess. Ask Him to reveal the pride that stands in His way and surrender it.

How amazing is it to have the creator of the Universe interested in you and your pain?

"BUT YOU, O GOD, ARE MY KING FROM LONG AGO; YOU BRING SALVATION UPON THE EARTH. IT WAS YOU WHO SPLIT OPEN THE SEAS BY YOUR POWER; YOU BROKE THE HEADS OF THE MONSTER IN THE WATERS. IT WAS YOU WHO CRUSHED THE HEADS OF LEVIATHAN AND GAVE HIM AS FOOD TO THE CREATURES OF THE DESERT. IT WAS YOU WHO OPEN SPRINGS AND STREAMS; YOU DRIED UP THE EVER-FLOWING RIVERS. THE DAY IS YOURS AND YOURS ALSO THE NIGHT; YOU ESTABLISHED THE SUN AND MOON. IT WAS YOU WHO SET ALL THE BOUNDARIES OF THE EARTH; YOU MADE BOTH SUMMER AND WINTER."

Psalm 74:12-17

CHAPTER EIGHTEEN

HEALING AFTER
DESTRUCTION
dana rodrigue

The struggle to want nothing else but to no longer be here is something I never thought I'd be released from. To shed darkness, fear, and depression is something only God did with me. That happens when we release it all to Him—and I mean ALL to Him.

I didn't realize until I was in my thirties that part of me died at a very young age. When my mother divorced my alcoholic father, I was two years old. My hopes and dreams of having a father were stripped away. By the time I was five years old, my innocence was taken from me and seeds of sexual doubt were planted. This brought confusion and anger within me. The sexual abuse carried on throughout my teenage years, which gave those negative seeds power and control over my thoughts and worth. I knew deep down it wasn't right; I felt dirty. I was trapped in this cycle of molestation that led to no self-worth. This cycle filled my heart with so much pain. I got married young, became a mother, and shoved the pain down deep ignoring it as most mothers, women, and wives do.

Alcohol became my medicine. The numbing sensation was a relief, until eventually it wasn't enough anymore. My struggles, pain, and coping cost me everything. I continued to learn that burying all my pain and self-medicating tricked my brain to believe the lies that I wasn't enough. I felt unworthy and not a "good enough" momma. I was so far in my mess that I believed my daughter would be better off without me. So I signed my rights over to her father, whom I knew would take care of her.

Fatherless. Childless. Friendless. I was invisible to everyone. No one could hear my silent scream for help. I continued to die inside. I needed a release from the pain, loneliness, and darkness, so I cut. I turned my abdomen into my battlefield.

I felt unloved and forgotten, although I mastered a fake smile to fool the world. Not dealing with the pain correctly led me into a toxic and verbally abusive marriage. I had another child and the cycle repeated itself. Except this marriage killed every last shred of who I was as a woman, a mother, and a person. I laid in bed night after night, knowing I wasn't his only woman. My body no longer met his standards.

I wanted the torment to end. I believed the only choice was to end my life to rid myself of the agonizing pain deep within my heart, soul, and mind. The day I took an entire bottle of narcotics is a blur. I remember waking up in the hospital and looking around; a small part of me hoped my husband would care enough to even be there. He wasn't.

I knew then I had to make a change. It was obvious God kept me breathing for a purpose. Over time I picked up pieces of my life. Baby steps and tiny pieces, but I cared enough to pick them up. I handed Him each piece, "Do what YOU want with them, Lord. You are my only HOPE." I was tired. I felt I didn't give Him much to work with. But He did. Oh, did He ever.

Sitting in my pastor's office, he told me, "Give God six months of your life and watch what He will do." I was too emotionally thinned out to even think of handing over my heart in the hands of another, but God knew I needed to understand unconditional love not just in the spirit but also in the natural. Six months later, I hired an electrician for some home repairs. The moment I met him, I knew something was different about him.

I continued my six month commitment with Jesus, but cutting was still a part of my story. It was a negative coping skill that I needed healing and freedom from. When someone turns to cutting, it's because they need to feel the pain release that's been bottled up from inside. I remember sitting in the tub full of bloody water when I heard a knock on the door. It was Patrick, the electrician. God told him to come to my house. We hadn't gone on a date or anything like that up to this point. When I realized it was him at the door, I tried to clean up the mess, but it was too late. He walked in. I burst into tears, weeping from the pit of my soul. He stood me up, wrapped me in a towel and brought me to the bed. He butterflied my deep cuts and cleaned me up. He cleaned the entire bathroom. Patrick was the first man I ever knew that took care of a wound rather than putting them there.

Fast forward, he asked for my hand in marriage and made me a mom again to his five-year-old son. God taught me I am valued and my life was worth something greater than I could comprehend. I continued to give God my pieces, and He continued to mold my healing.

Years later, I had to have a surgery to remove a ball of tissue under my belly button that formed from a complication of a previous surgery. During my consult, my doctor asked me if I had any previous surgeries because of all my scarring. I didn't want to tell how they got there, but answered, "Years ago I was a self cutter and my abdomen was my area of choice." Dr. DeLatte said, "I tell you what, I am going to cut you from hip to hip, fix this ball of tissue but I am also going to pull your skin down and remove every single one of these scars."

I was in disbelief! I sat up and said, "Do you mean I won't have ANY hate scars when this is over!?" He said, "You sure won't." I can't tell you the shock my husband and I were both in. Two years later we're still in amazement of God's cleansing grace! That was a God moment I will NEVER forget!!

God has not only used the shredded, bruised, and nearly dead pieces to heal me. He brought my first-born back, restored my marriage, gave me a son, but most important restored me as His daughter. Knowing who I am in Him brings me new reasons to live, and for that I am forever grateful.

DEVOTION
andrea bourgeois

Destruction to our land by storms left our people feeling hopeless. The overwhelming thoughts of how this can ever get better seem daunting and out of arm's reach. Waking up and seeing the devastation day after day, opens the wounds and keeps us trapped in our own thoughts. The feelings of hopelessness take over and blind us from seeing God and His helping hand.

Self-destruction does the same thing. When someone is in the thick of it, they can't see past that moment. The weight of their despair presses down and keeps them stuck in a state of depression. The thoughts and feelings that what they are facing will never get better causes their minds to go deeper into how to make this pain stop. Waking up to the realization of self-hate or self-destruction paralyzes our brains, and we cannot think outside of our box.

God wants to heal our land and heal our bodies, our minds, and our souls.

Do you see destruction and feel there's no way out? Are you hopeless in your situation? Are you seeking for a release of your pain?

Look up to our heavenly Father and seek His face. Reach out to someone! Ask for help while praying for God to restore you and your land. He will make it better than you left it.

"IF MY PEOPLE, WHO ARE CALLED BY MY NAME, WILL HUMBLE THEMSELVES AND PRAY AND SEEK MY FACE AND TURN FROM THEIR WICKED WAYS, THEN WILL I HEAR FROM HEAVEN AND WILL FORGIVE THEIR SIN AND WILL HEAL THEIR LAND."

2 Chronicles 7:14

CHAPTER NINETEEN

EYES OF
FAITH
michelle rabon

The sound of the cars colliding was deafening. Yet in that moment, the impact seemed to bring my world to a silent pause. There was no noise when the car finally came to the stop. One moment I was listening to the laughter of my children, the next moment the world was quiet.

Nothing prepares you for moments like these, moments that will be epically etched into the hardwiring of your memory. Moments that will quickly change the landscape of how you live your life. When I turned around, I saw that my children were OK, they were alive, I was alive. Moments like that change us because God gave us the chance to live.

In the weeks that pressed on after the accident, the pain and bruises left behind reminded me of God's protection. But more than that, God used them to remind me of all He had done in my life. God's redemption and transformation that had taken place several years earlier had become bland because I had become careless.

I wasted so much time just going through life, not serving Him.

I spent my time being broken and trying to fill the gaps in my own strength and not God's.

In the years leading to the accident, I lost my fire and my passion. I lost my desire to serve. I sought everything but the Word.

Truth be told I had put Him on my unimportant list. Everything else became more important than the One who changed it all for me. After the accident, I knew that God allowed me the chance to make a fresh commitment, a commitment that would never fade with time. The accident became a promise to God that no matter what, I would seek and serve Him every day.

God kept reminding me of Paul's words in 2 Corinthians 12:9 when he said, "But He said to me, 'My grace is sufficient for you, for my power is made perfect in weakness.' Therefore, I will boast all the more gladly of my weaknesses, so that the power of Christ may rest upon me." (ESV). My greatest weaknesses were my unwillingness to give up control, my lack of desire to study His Word, and my failure to pray. Each one of these was keeping me from being what God needed me to be.

The beauty is, when we hand over our weaknesses to our faithful Father, He can turn them into usable strengths through His power, through His Spirit. Areas of my life I never thought I would hand over to the Father have become the strengths He has used to build my ministry and to reach women with His Word. In our weaknesses is where He is strong.

Nothing is too hard for God; not even our greatest weaknesses.

God brought me to a desperate place. A place where my weakness seemed far greater than His strength. I needed His Word to wash deep over me, but my unworthy thoughts created an impossible view when I sat down to His powerful Word. I could hear God nudge, "Just open it, and I will provide for you."

When I opened His Word, I began slowly to unlock with renewed vision what God himself needed me to see. He crushed the doubts and awakened the suppressed spirit within me because I was now tapping into His life source; I was drawing from the well. I saw the transformation of what opening His word would do; not just for me as a wife, a mother, and a woman, but as a loved, called, redeemed child of the living God. The greatest lesson of my life came in the darkest time in my spiritual journey.

The journey away from the darkest places in my life began by simply opening His Word. My dry soul needed water--living water, from the living Word. Friend, nothing in this life is too great for our incredible God, even when we feel like we cannot see His plan.

When I sat at the feet of Jesus through the book of John a few months into this journey of His Word, I read of the blind man. The man that Jesus touched and gave sight so the grace of God would be displayed upon him. I may not have been literally blind, but I was spiritually blind before I gave my life to Christ when I was nineteen. God restored my spiritual sight so I would display His grace.

I needed God to show me that in this dark place He had a plan that when He changed my life all those years ago; He didn't do it by mistake. When I trusted Him as my savior many years ago, He knew I would be in this season transformed by His power. He wants to display His grace in me and through me. Grace that is messy and not perfect, grace that leaves evidence of itself everywhere it goes not because of who I am but because of who He is and the work He is doing within me.

God has radical, grace-filled plans for your life—plans to bring you to a place where you will drip with His grace every step you take. Our purpose may be far beyond what we can see right now in the dark place we are in, but God sees us there. He meets us there and grace begins by opening His Word and letting Him provide the rest.

There is no darkness too great for Jesus. There are no depths to low or high He cannot reach us.

After my accident I had a choice to make, I had to choose between the pain I was feeling externally and the pain I was feeling internally. Focusing on the external pain wouldn't change my internal problem. Which one was I willing to hand over to God? Was I willing to give Him the deepest places that longed so deeply for Him, even if it felt too impossible? Was I willing to place my hands in His and allow Him to lead me rather than it just being halfway?

God in His infinite wisdom knew the choice I needed to make, and He waited patiently for me.

He is waiting patiently for you; He is waiting gently for you to see your unquenchable need for Him. You and I are the blind man in John 9, and He is seeking to restore our sight and display His grace in us.

DEVOTION

andrea bourgeois

After a powerful storm, the landscape changes and the buildings are destroyed. Driving into our hometown after Hurricane Laura was heartbreaking to see all the trees down and roofs of homes and businesses ripped off. Trees snapped in half or uprooted laid flat all over the terrain. This war-zone look has been etched into our brains forever. It's a scar that will tell a heart wrenching story for years to come.

Our storms in our lives leave scars, too. These scars heal but remain so we can comfort others as God comforted us.

If we focus too much on the destruction or the pain, we lose sight of what God is trying to teach and do in our lives. Like Paul, he needed new eyes to see the world and his life as God wanted him to. It says in Acts, "Immediately, something like scales fell from Saul's eyes, and he could see again. He got up and was baptized, and after taking some food, he regained his strength."

We read God's word as our daily bread. We fill up on God's food and nourishment, then we regain strength with God as our Strength Provider.

Are you blinded by the destruction surrounding you? Do you dwell in your situation and put your focus on the negative and the pain you are facing? Have you gone to Christ as your sole provider for the right food for nourishment and for new eyes? Are your eyes covered in scales of the negativity of others and of the world?

Ask God for new eyes to see your struggle in a new light. He is there ready to reveal His plans and direction for you.

After our scales are removed—our fear, our pain, and our crushed and grieving dreams—we can see again. We refocus and renew our love to our Heavenly Father and then we eat to regain our strength. The mess and destruction won't look so daunting when we look at it through Jesus' eyes. We'll see areas for improvement and ways to restore what was once destroyed. We'll see the openings God is creating for us instead of the closed doors surrounding us.

IMMEDIATELY, SOMETHING LIKE SCALES FELL FROM SAUL'S EYES, AND HE COULD SEE AGAIN. HE GOT UP AND WAS BAPTIZED, AND AFTER TAKING SOME FOOD, HE REGAINED HIS STRENGTH."

Acts 9:18-19

CHAPTER TWENTY

---ONE DAY AT A---
TIME
ryan clemons

My journey began when I discovered I was a pregnant at nineteen. It upset my parents, especially my dad. He was so disturbed he kicked me out and sold my car. During the next three years, I moved seven to nine times with my son. It was a stressful time. And for three years my dad didn't speak to me. The crazy part is, we went to the same church. He would sit on his side of the pew, and I would sit on my side, and he would walk past me like I didn't exist. It was very hurtful to be ignored by my dad. So, I prayed this same prayer for three years, asking God to soften my dad's heart.

I went back to college at McNeese State University while working three part-time jobs. One day I was at the civic center, and saw my entire family, mom, dad, and two younger sisters. My mom encouraged me to give my dad a hug. I was hesitant because I didn't think he'd hug me back. I finally summoned courage, and I wrapped my arms around him with the biggest hug I could give. And guess what happened? My dad hugged me back. We exchanged no words, but tears flowed from both of us. It was there we both felt the love and grace of forgiveness.

I forgave my dad for not being there for me and all the people that treated me like I was damaged goods. I had to realize forgiveness was not for them. It was for me, and I had to free myself from bondage. When I surrendered all of my struggles to God, He worked wondrously in my life. I graduated from college on time with my class with a Bachelor of Science in Mass Communication and Public Relations. I'm currently working on my Master's in Counseling and Development.

After my experience, God placed a vision in my heart to write a book, hoping to minister to other single moms. So, I said yes to God's will, and in 2016 I wrote a book called Victorious: The Journey of a Single Mom and Her Faith. God also allowed me to meet, partner, and collaborate with Mrs. Aline Pires, the founder of Pink Life. She had a vision of helping single moms and decreasing the number of teen pregnancies. Her vision aligned with my personal hardships in life, and I created a program called Pink Girls, a mentoring program for young girls ages eleven to eighteen. Pink Girls would be a preventive measure to decrease the number of teen pregnancies. I wrote a curriculum for elementary, middle, and high school girls, and I chose different topics relevant to the average girl. The topics include self-esteem, inner beauty, self-respect, boundaries, dating, girl drama, bullying, positive changes, and more! At this point, I felt if I can help a young girl make better decisions and not becoming a teen mom, then I've done my job. This would be my contribution to Pink Life, and this is how God had turned my pain into purpose. I also wrote a curriculum for single moms, which includes topics such as heart check, accountability, setting goals, self-esteem, overcoming doubts and fears, purpose, and so much more! I wrote the curriculum because I felt like single moms could use another support system. God had so many beautiful plans birthed from my pain, and it was all because I said, "Yes!" I want to share my key tips to living a victorious life and putting your pain into perspective.

Building a "New You" starts with recognizing your imperfections and acknowledging the areas you need to improve on. This also means turning away from that negative behavior or behaviors to move forward and stepping into what God has called you to be.

ACCOUNTABILITY: Taking ownership and responsibility of yourself and admitting when you're wrong, even when it's hard. When you take ownership of your flaws and imperfections, that takes power away from someone trying to hold that information over your head.

SETTING PERSONAL AND FAMILY GOALS: Create family time, family meetings, and/or family fun. It's important to have honest and real conversations with your family to gain different perspectives and check in with each other.

ACTION PLAN: Create steps for your action plan by creating timelines, deadlines, and realistic goals that are attainable and eventually grow into bigger goals.

OVERCOMING DOUBTS AND FEARS: The enemy likes to plant seeds of negative reminders of our past, but God forgave us a long time ago. It's important to speak the word of God in your heart and your mind. This will also take prayer, community, and a personal support system to help you step out of your comfort zone.

SELF-MOTIVATION: A great activity to help with self-esteem is writing positive sayings and acknowledging the noble qualities about you. For example, I am enough. I am beautiful, I am smart. You can post these sticky notes on your mirror or your door as a reminder when you're having hard days or experiencing negative thoughts.

SELF-LOVE: Make more time to refuel and refresh; this will allow you to be beneficial to your family.

PURPOSE: To know your purpose in life, then reflect on your life and ask yourself what comes naturally, easily and what brings fulfillment in your life?

STANDING IN YOUR TRUTH: Be open and honest about your journey in life with others. When you share your story, this allows you to be a part of someone's healing.

BOLD AND BRAVE: Say yes!! There are masses of people waiting for your boldness and bravery.

DEVOTION
andrea bourgeois

Clean up after a storm takes time. It's a slow and steady race or marathon that seems daunting when you're standing in all destruction. I was raking leaves, branches, roofing shingles, and other random debris like Styrofoam insulation and metal building pieces a few days after the hurricane for multiple days. I was dripping sweat from my head to my toes. I had a heat rash around my ankles because the heat was trapped in my rubber boots, and all I had was ankle no-show running socks. I found leg warmers and put those on my lower legs to keep the boots from rubbing blisters on my calves and shins. Mosquito bites were all over my scraped and scratched prickly legs, and my clothes were drenched in sweat, as was my hair in a messy bun. My shoulders were burning in the sun and aching from being overworked in the same motion from raking and sweeping.

My husband came up to me and said, "Why don't you take a break? It's not a race, Andrea. Nice and steady wins the race. Babe, we'll get it all cleaned up; it will take us some time, though. Just focus on one little area so you can sit back and see the progress to celebrate that bit of cleaned-up green grass or flower beds. Don't get a heat stroke out here. It will be here tomorrow and the next day, so take it easy a bit." as he handed me a jug of ice-cold water and Powerade mixed. Ahh, and that quenched my thirst and my soul!

In our storms of life, God gives us this promise to approach His throne for help in our time of need. We have to pace ourselves and find a rhythm in seeking God for help. We can't get out of our mess overnight. We can try running from it, but when we come back home - it's still there waiting on us to clean it up.

When we learn to seek His throne for help, we learn to focus on a little patch or area in our mess at a time. Slowly with God's help, we'll

138

get it all cleaned up and restored. It's a long hard process, but it's doable. We'll have inconveniences and issues that pop up, but we'll survive them in the storm we face.

WE'LL MAKE IT THROUGH THE RAIN.

Are you trying to clean up your mess on your own? Have you approached His throne for help? Are you the rabbit racing to get out of your struggle, or are you the slow and steady tortoise working a little bit each day to accomplish the ultimate goal?

God wants to grant us grace and mercy, especially in our time of need! One day at a time, seek Him for His direction, His pace, and His peace.

"LET US THEN APPROACH THE THRONE OF GRACE WITH CONFIDENCE SO THAT WE MAY RECEIVE MERCY AND FIND GRACE TO HELP US IN OUR TIME OF NEED."

Hebrews 4: 16

CHAPTER TWENTY-ONE

—DRY BONES IN THE—
VALLEY
crystal mayo

"WHAT NO EYE HAS SEEN, WHAT NO EAR HAS HEARD, AND WHAT NO HUMAN MIND HAS CONCEIVED"— THE THINGS GOD HAS PREPARED FOR THOSE WHO LOVE HIM—" *1 Corinthians 2:9.*

One of my favorite Bibles belonged to my grandmother. It contains many promises and prayers for our family. I added "Homeschooling 2016-17" next to the verse above. I felt confident that the Lord was moving me from children's ministry service into the season of homeschooling my three children. But I was soon reminded that my plans are not always His.

One morning, before the homeschooling phase was to begin, I babysat for my fellow homeschooling friend. But the time had ended sooner than I had expected. What began as a headache became so severe and disorienting that I could not supervise her children. Even after days of rest, my headache, nausea, and dizziness continued. My doctor's initial diagnosis was vertigo. That led to a prescription medication which only made me extremely sleepy. You can imagine with three young children at home, it's difficult for Mom to take personal days! So, feeling that something wasn't right, I put out a post asking for prayers, then got down on my knees and asked the Lord for help and guidance before I took a nap. I was exhausted.

When I awoke from my sleep, it became clear there was an issue. I toppled out of the bed, face down on the floor. I yelled for my husband Doug, and he helped me to the chair. My blood pressure reading was high. It was late, and he wanted me to get back in bed; I knew rest wasn't helping. I insisted he take me to the hospital. He agreed and carried me, along with our sleepy children, to the car. Doug's parents graciously kept our kids so we could get some answers.

During the night, a CT scan and a few tests were taken but showed nothing abnormal. The doctor on call concluded that I was having anxiety. I thought, "Yeah, you would have anxiety if you couldn't walk." As they released me, I questioned the nurse again and again. Can this really be anxiety? Do you really think I should go home? But he deferred to the doctor's decision as he wheeled me out to the car ramp.

Wanting a second opinion, we drove two hours west to Houston. I was admitted on a Sunday afternoon and early that next morning at 1:00 a.m. a doctor woke me to tell me I had experienced a major stroke. It shocked me. I was only thirty-eight years old. Why was I having a stroke? Through tears, I turned to the Lord. I opened my hands and said, "Lord?" I immediately felt His presence on my right side as He spoke, saying, "I will restore you." I knew that God does not lie. Still, it would take great faith to believe when I could not see.

After eighteen days of evaluation by medical experts, they discovered paralysis on my left side and partial blindness in both eyes, along with short term memory and sensory processing issues. I had a hard time multitasking with simple skills. Once we returned home, our kids went back to public school. This allowed me to go to therapy, doctor appointments, and rest throughout the day. I didn't drive for two years, and that's when our church and family stepped in. They helped us with prayer, transportation, or meals.

Venturing out in public brought on panic attacks. I would weep uncontrollably when things got too hard. I lived in fear of everything and soon felt like a prisoner in my home. Anxiety medication helped me cope and enabled me to walk outside to greet my kids as they got off the school bus each day. When people would see me fall apart, I just hated it. But that's when God would remind me, in my weakness, He is strong.

I became a desperate woman in need of healing. I related to the woman with an issue of blood in the Bible. Matthew 9:20-22 says, "Just then a woman who had been subject to bleeding for twelve years came up behind him and touched the edge of his cloak. She said to herself, 'If I only touch his cloak, I will be healed.' Jesus turned and saw her. 'Take heart, daughter,' he said, 'your faith has healed you.' And the woman was healed at that moment." She had seen so many doctors, but none could heal her.

I understood why she reached out to Jesus. He could have let her walk away, but He acknowledged her and the healing. I wanted that too! I went into my closet and took out one of Doug's t-shirts and hung it up in front of me. I placed a pair of his sandals down below the shirt. I sat there imagining I was sitting at the feet of Jesus. I told him everything I was feeling; I held nothing back. I clung to the hem of that t-shirt and surrendered it all to Him. Everything. The pain, the disappointment, all of it. I asked Him to restore me just like He promised He would in that hospital room two years prior.

That was the day things turned around. The weeping stopped immediately and other things progressively. Gradually, the doctors took me off most prescription drugs. It was a miracle that I didn't need them anymore. Instead, I took the communion daily, thanking Him for the body and the blood He shed for me on the cross. I proclaimed that by His stripes I am healed. He restored my vision and the ability to drive. He gave me tools to fight fear with faith and how-to live-in freedom.

As I am writing this, today marks four years since the stroke. It surprises people to learn that I was ever ill. God completely rebuilt, restored, and renewed my life. God had kept His promise from 1 Corinthians 2:9. We weren't able to walk through those homeschool doors, but He has opened other doors of ministry where I can share my story of hope with others. It's true the journey looked different than what we thought, but no eye could see what God had planned for us. This is when I began to see crystal clear.

DEVOTION
andrea bourgeois

In this life we have trouble. We aren't exempt from trials, storms, and heartaches. When our world begins to shatter and fall apart, God sees the beauty that will come from the ashes. Our lives, our homes, our bodies and our careers can be destroyed and yet we must look up and see that Heaven is closer than we can see. He won't forsake us. He can take a valley of dry bones and breathe life back into them to give them more life than they had before.

Sometimes we've been beaten down so many times that we believe the lies from the enemy that we're nothing. We believe the lies that God doesn't love us or we're unlovable. Our valley of dry bones can result from years of abuse or disease, of decades of financial hardships or burdens, or of months of isolation and heartaches. The weight we carry on our shoulders wears us down over time; we weren't created to carry that weight alone. But, God says to our dry bones, "I will make breath enter you and you will come to life!"

What has slowly been smothering you? Are you battling an illness? Have you lost everything? Are you standing in the valley looking out in desperation? Do you feel you have nothing left?

God can speak to your dry bones and breathe life back into whatever situation you are in. He hears you. He sees you. He loves you. And He wants you to cry out to Him to revive your dry bones.

"PROPHESY TO THESE BONES AND SAY TO THEM, 'DRY
BONES, HEAR THE WORD OF THE LORD! THIS IS WHAT
THE SOVEREIGN LORD SAYS TO THESE BONES: I WILL
MAKE BREATH ENTER YOU AND YOU WILL COME TO LIFE.
I WILL ATTACH TENDONS TO YOU AND MAKE FLESH
COME UPON YOU AND COVER YOU WITH SKIN; I WILL
PUT BREATH IN YOU, AND YOU WILL COME TO LIFE.
THEN YOU KNOW THAT I AM THE LORD.'"

Ezekiel 37: 4-6

CHAPTER TWENTY-TWO

—— CHOOSE TO ——
BELIEVE
marlisa harding

Church hurt is one of the worst hurts. Perhaps this is because it's unexpected, fraught with plausible excuses or filled with people who are supposed to be "above it." Or perhaps it's because deep down you often know the culprits are unintentional and unknowing of the depths of their blows?

I fell deeply in love with Jesus at a young age, and a close second love was my home church, a Body to this day that I still hold in high regard. I can confidently say this now because I am past the pain and I truly know that learning broken theology, and the natural repercussions of these lessons, are only to be blamed on the broken state of a humanity that tries its best to convey their understanding of God.

Growing up, I learned that our words are powerful; "Death and life are in the power of the tongue" (Proverbs 18:21) and that if you "Say unto this mountain be thou removed" (Mark 11:23) it will happen. These are truths I still believe today. They are the Word of God. But the application, the context, the finitude of humanity, and the infinite sovereignty of God were lessons I had to learn the hard way.

And honestly, I think it was all for the best.

I was miserable at work. It was a good job with benefits and a future I was on a fast track to get. But it was Plan B. All along I knew that was the case, like going up on a rollercoaster knowing the drop was coming. But it wasn't until I caught a glimpse of myself in my dream job that I knew I could never go back to Plan B.

I did all of the natural things to nail the job. I had the exact college degree, five years of experience, a flawless resume, prepared a PowerPoint for the interview, and even bought a new outfit.

I did all of the supernatural things too--all of the things I was told were necessary to get God to work. I gave a special offering. I ran around my car and marched in front of the office gate in step with praise music like it was my Jericho and my victory was on the other side of the wall. I got up early for weeks to pray and declare the job was mine, giving thanks to God it was already done.

But I didn't get the job.

Crushed and angry at myself for getting my hopes up, frustrated that I was forever changed knowing my heart could never go back to Plan B (despite my body showing up for work each day), I was highly upset with God. "He'd failed me," I thought. I did all the stuff I was supposed to do but He didn't do his part.

Though I was angry with God, I kept speaking to Him. Stubbornly and with an attitude, I let him know how I felt because I didn't want to just break things off. And then He spoke:

"You had more faith in your works than in my ability to do the job."

And there it was—twenty-five years of theology down the toilet. I knew He was right. And just like I knew I couldn't go back to Plan B for work, I knew that faith in my own works was a faulty theology that could never be mine again.

That was the lesson to be learned. It was never about the job.It was about discovering who God was and how He wanted to commune with me as a Father and not a genie.

Not getting the job changed the way I prayed for myself and for others. It changed the way I spoke about God and His word, and it changed my approach to trials. Perhaps the victory promised us isn't about getting to the perceived other side? Perhaps it's about getting to a new depth, a new understanding and a new relationship with the Father?

I've learned this lesson quite vividly in my relationship with my mother. Our relationship has always been tense. For years I wrestled with myself, God, my mother, and even unintentionally with other people regarding why our relationship couldn't be what all that I'd hoped it to be. I thought the "victory" meant we would become some storybook or sitcom version of the perfect mother/daughter.

AND THAT IS WHERE MY HEALING CAME.

By focusing on myself, leaving my mother out of my emotional space while still trusting the Lord with the outcome, I found wholeness.

Wholeness: Something I never thought to pray for myself.

My words, my brain, my declarations never knew that's what I needed. Yet that's what I found when I let God be Lord over the situation.

Things might change. They might not. But it doesn't matter anymore. I am me. I am well and I am whole.

I think that's what the Lord wanted me to see. While we think we're working or convincing Him to do something, He's writing a whole different story. A story that is complete and perfect because He is the author and the finisher.

Now I pray for that. "Lord, what are you teaching? What are you showing me? I am listening no matter how long it takes."

DEVOTION
andrea bourgeois

Standing in debris and uprooted trees looking up at our hundred-year-old home, I noticed all the missing shingles and siding along with sections of the outer walls and roof caving in from our storage room and my husband's woodworking shop. My heart broke in so many ways. I felt overwhelmed. Then hearing how some of our friends lost their entire home and everything in it or their businesses, I felt more overwhelmed. Seeing the mess and destruction of all the power lines and power poles, I continued to feel overwhelmed. Crying with my friend on my in-laws' back patio while slapping mosquitoes as we watched our husbands tarp our roof, I felt overwhelmed. But then God rescued me in my moments of despair when He sent me a message through a friend's text that night that read, "I have to keep reminding myself He can be nothing but faithful! Believe with me!"

Saturday, August 29, 2020, was the day I nailed a stake down to no longer live in doubt with all this hurricane related pain and sorrow. Instead, I would stand firm and believe that when it looks impossible, that's when God makes things possible!

Are you struggling with believing that God hears your cries and pain? Do you believe He is faithful? Do you believe He will make a way when there's no way? Have you rebuked and repented the doubt that's keeping you from seeing God move mountains in your life right now?

Drive a stake down today as you rebuke the doubt and believe God has a plan and a way out for you! Just because He doesn't answer the way we think He should, doesn't mean He's not working! Our Almighty God is not a genie. His ways are always higher!

That's all that is required of us. He wants us to just BELIEVE Him and hold on to the hope He is and always will be faithful.

THEN JESUS SAID TO THOMAS, "PUT YOUR FINGER HERE; SEE MY HANDS. REACH OUT YOUR HAND AND PUT IT INTO MY SIDE. STOP DOUBTING AND BELIEVE."

John 20: 27

"THEN JESUS SAID, 'DID I NOT TELL YOU THAT IF YOU BELIEVED, YOU WOULD SEE THE GLORY OF GOD?'"

John 11: 40

CHAPTER TWENTY-THREE

ROOTED

lisa jones

I'LL NEVER FORGET THE MOMENT I WALKED INTO MY HOUSE TO FIND THAT NOTHING WAS IN ITS PLACE.

I wouldn't call myself a domestic queen, by any stretch of the imagination. I'm creative but the art of homemaking is challenging for me. I'm fantastic at making messes; it's like one of my superpowers. But this? This was far beyond any mess I'd ever made.

Growing up in a house with all organized personalities, I stood out as the sporadic, messy one and was often referred to as hurricane Lisa. For once, I was not the mess-making culprit. This was an actual hurricane named Katrina.

It appeared the contents of our home had been thrown into a blender full of nasty water on the high-speed milkshake setting and spewed back. The refrigerator was making a bridge across our shotgun kitchen where it landed and wedged itself after floating in the floodwater. It was a chaotic sight to see.

A church team arrived from another state to help. Greeting them, I jokingly requested they excuse my housekeeping skills. Thirteen labor intensive hours later, with the soaking wet, mildewed contents of our home strewn in the yard, we said goodbye and they prayed with us, commenting on our peace and ability to work and joke in the face of such disaster. Only Jesus.

In hindsight, I realize that our unshakeable faith in God as our provider with an assurance that He was working all things for our good did not come because of an instantaneous decision to have extreme faith in an unseen God amidst a hopeless situation.

Rather, a response of faith bloomed like a flower in the wake of disaster because of years of planting consistent seeds of faith in our hearts. The soil of our hearts where the seeds lay dormant had been cultivated by the consistent hearing of the Word of God. The storm rushed in and flooded the soil, but the roots were in a firm foundation. Those seeds weren't ruined and didn't wash away like our earthly possessions did that day.

The aftermath of the storm brought many hard moments; not all of them handled with such grace. Every moment was an opportunity to choose between faith and trust. Everything felt out of control. Thankfully, we knew God was in control.

We clung to faith that gave us confidence and hope. A domino effect of getting outside our comfort zones, many learning opportunities, and a huge faith walk would follow. God's peace that passes all understanding showed up again and again

In the months to follow, I felt as though there was a seesaw in my mind with control sitting on one side and trust on the other. Whichever one I fed would win. When control won the seesaw battle, it gave the prideful illusion of being grounded. I felt more out of control than ever. When trust won, I felt safe with a peaceful reassurance that everything would be OK even if I didn't understand how.

On one of the many monotonous days to follow during the emotional marathon of dragging everything into the yard, I stood there like a deer in headlights contemplating this mountain of decisions in front of me. I looked down at my "frumpy in-between regular clothes and maternity clothes" outfit and sighed. I walked around the pile, picking up some of my favorites. My eyes landed on maternity clothes with tags, and I shook my head. I'd tried them on and found them awkward and too big, but I would need some soon. Running my hand along the hem of one of my favorite dresses, I wondered, "What if I can't find clothes I love and can afford? What if we can barely buy essentials? How will we ever replace all of this?"

I knew God was calling me to lean not on my understanding, but be thankful and trust Him to make our path straight. We certainly had our lives to be thankful for.

God taught us trust, even when our insurance didn't replace these material possessions. What looked hopeless from one perspective was an enormous opportunity from another. It was an internal struggle, but the beginning of an enriching journey of learning how to exchange my fearful what if questions for learning to trust God more.

It was an eye-opening realization of how God's ways are not our ways. The seesaw of control and trust taught me I could determine which one I was grounded in by the type of questions I asked and how I looked at things. If I consumed myself with worry and what if questions, my need for control grew. When I trusted God, speaking faith over circumstances that didn't look the way I wanted, my trust and faith grew.

We saw so many miracles come out of this storm. Many were spontaneous and material. However, most of the miracles were in the transformation of our worries and fears that blossomed slowly through our faith walk and daily choices of trusting God.

Most of the time those transformational miracles are only visible in the rear view. My journal from these years is full of them. When we write it down, we prepare a beautiful record of God's redemption to look back on. This allows us a visual measure of progress and builds our faith for new challenges ahead.

Jimmy Needham has a song I love entitled "I Need You Like a Hurricane." In the song, he sings about needing Jesus to be like a hurricane and tear his walls down. Looking back in hindsight and through my journals, I reflect on our journey of faith over the last decade and a half since Hurricane Katrina. I am reminded of our perspective change and growth opportunities those circumstances afforded us. Considering all this, I am so very grateful that hurricane tore my walls down.

lisa jones

DEVOTION
andrea bourgeois

What kind of soil has your faith been cultivating in? Will flood waters or high winds push your seeds of faith away? Or after the waters reside and the winds die down, are your seeds still there? How rooted in Christ are you?

"Listen then to what the parable of the sower means: When anyone hears the message about the kingdom and does not understand it, the evil one comes and snatches away what was sown in their heart. This is the seed sown along the path. The seed falling on rocky ground refers to someone who hears the word and at once receives it with joy. But since they have no root, they last only a short time. When trouble or persecution comes because of the word, they fall away. The seed falling among the thorns refers to someone who hears the word, but the worries of this life and the deceitfulness of wealth choke the word, making it unfruitful. But the seed falling on good soil refers to someone who hears the word and understands it. This is the one who produces a crop, yielding a hundred, sixty or thirty times what was sown." Matthew 13:8

Many times, we struggle to bounce back from a hardship or a struggle because our faith has been sown in shallow, weedy or dry soil. Our hearts can become hard if we don't allow Jesus to quench our thirst. Our faith can get lost in our hearts if we have tons of weeds growing, choking out the sunlight and nutrients. And we can lose faith if our ground is rocky and the roots are shallow, they can't withstand the heat or storms.

Watching our community come together and rebuild reminds me of why I love being from southwest Louisiana. We truly are "Tuff in the Bluff," and SWLA STRONG is more than a hashtag. It's a way of life!

What kind of soil do you have? What can you do to get your soil enriched with nutrients from the Lord so your roots can grow deep into the soil?

"THEN JESUS TOLD THEM MANY THINGS IN PARABLES, SAYING: 'A FARMER WENT OUT TO SOW HIS SEED. AS HE WAS SCATTERING THE SEED, SOME FELL ALONG THE PATH, AND THE BIRDS CAME AND ATE IT UP. SOME FELL ON ROCKY PLACES, WHERE IT HAD LITTLE SOIL. IT SPRANG UP QUICKLY BECAUSE THE SOIL WAS SHALLOW. BUT WHEN THE SUN CAME UP, THE PLANTS WERE SCORCHED, AND THEY WITHERED BECAUSE THEY HAD NO ROOT. OTHER SEED FELL AMONG THORNS, WHICH GREW UP AND CHOKED THE PLANTS. STILL OTHER SEED FELL ON GOOD SOIL, WHERE IT PRODUCED A CROP—A HUNDRED, SIXTY OR THIRTY TIMES WHAT WAS SOWN.'"

Matthew 13:18-23

CHAPTER TWENTY-FOUR

A NEW
START
ainsley britain

Have you ever seen a butterfly pop out of its cocoon and dry its wings in the wind? The insect that was once one thing transforms into another, and as soon as it emerges, you can see the change.

I never thought I'd compare myself to an insect. Still, an identity shift image is where I'd like to invite you as we enter the healing story that made me new.

I will never forget a moment with Jesus, two days after I experienced my first real heartbreak. It was one of those heartbreaks where you lose your appetite, cannot get out of bed, and question your entire future. It was so excruciating. However, because God is good, He reminded me of some things.

When I could finally peel myself from my bed and out from under my comforter, I got in the car. I was driving around Nashville, seeing all the familiar places that suddenly had memories like ghosts dancing around them, as I faced a new reality.

The relationship I was in was toxic and abusive, which skewed the way I viewed myself and demolished my self-worth. I quit going to church, isolated myself from my friends, and was constantly defending my boyfriend to my family. This relationship defined me, and when it was ripped away from me, I fell flat on my face.

I couldn't tell you the last time I had spoken to Jesus when I got in that car, but something told me to turn the radio to K-LOVE radio. Worship music flooded my car, pouring healing from my speakers as a lump formed in my throat and tears ran down my cheeks. I began weeping. It was like breaking the silence of sadness with worship broke the enemy's lies, and a river washed over me. My words were utterly lost, and as I searched for more, all I could do was say, "Freedom."

A parking lot welcomed me as I pulled over because my own tears clouded my vision and, "Freedom" was the only word I could muster. Looking to my right and left in disbelief, my arms seemed to raise themselves without my knowledge! It's a good thing I pulled over! For a solid five minutes, I repeated the word "Freedom" in a place of pure, overwhelming worship.

Freedom from being mistreated and manipulated. Freedom from my old self. Freedom from the grip of negative comments on social media.

Unhealthy relationships lead to unhealthy heartbreak. The only way to recover from that is with Jesus and His radical healing.

As I type this, I glance down at my ring finger, where a shiny diamond sits as proof of God's healing and ultimately God's promise and plan for my life unfolding with a healthy, God-centered relationship with my incredible husband.

FREEDOM IN JESUS.

My identity was made new. I was no longer defined by an abusive boyfriend but by the Creator of the Universe who called me "worthy" and "loved." I felt like my heart was perfectly articulating what my whole body was feeling.

When Jesus moves, He moves in such a mighty and powerful way, sometimes you don't even know what's happening. After that day, I was so alive in Christ. A new, whole person emerged, and it was the most refreshing experience I've ever felt. Just me & Jesus, driving around Nashville. My friends and family noticed a difference right away, much like one does with a butterfly. I'll never forget that day. and all I could say was "FREEDOM."

DEVOTION
andrea bourgeois

After we get out of the storm, not only does God want us to pick up the pieces, but He wants us to move forward.

"FORGET THE FORMER THINGS AND DON'T DWELL IN THE PAST."

Yikes, this is hard sometimes. Our past changes us, but it does not define who we are any longer. We gain the freedom to live the life God has called us to out of whatever storm we may face.

What or where is He calling you out of in your life? Are you stuck looking back instead of looking forward to what God will do for you or in you?

He is doing something new in you, so try to celebrate the change from the hardships you are facing. Praise God for the change as He provides streams of water to drink and shelter along the way.

"SEE, I AM DOING A NEW THING!"

God rescues us! He provides a way out through the sea with a path through the mighty waters and tells us to not look back because He's doing a new thing!

"THIS IS WHAT THE LORD SAYS—
HE WHO MADE A WAY THROUGH THE SEA, A PATH THROUGH
THE MIGHTY WATERS, WHO DREW OUT THE CHARIOTS AND
HORSES, THE ARMY AND REINFORCEMENTS TOGETHER, AND
THEY LAY THERE, NEVER TO RISE AGAIN, EXTINGUISHED,
SNUFFED OUT LIKE A WICK: FORGET THE FORMER THINGS;
DO NOT DWELL ON THE PAST. SEE, I AM DOING A NEW THING!
NOW IT SPRINGS UP; DO YOU NOT PERCEIVE IT? I AM MAKING
A WAY IN THE WILDERNESS AND STREAMS IN THE WASTELAND.
THE WILD ANIMALS HONOR ME, THE JACKALS AND THE OWLS,
BECAUSE I PROVIDE WATER IN THE WILDERNESS AND STREAMS
IN THE WASTELAND, TO GIVE DRINK, TO MY PEOPLE, MY
CHOSEN, THE PEOPLE I FORMED FOR MYSELF THAT THEY MAY
PROCLAIM MY PRAISE."

Isaiah 43:16-21

CHAPTER TWENTY-FIVE

WHEN IT DOESN'T
MAKE SENSE
miranda vinson

Have you ever felt the nudging of the Holy Spirit moving you in a direction you had no desire to go?

That was me four years ago when I felt the Lord calling me to go back to college to get my master's degree. I had been teaching for ten years and I loved being in the classroom. It was my calling and ministry, and I was passionate about building relationships with my students.

So, when I felt the nudge to get my master's degree, I fought it. I did not want to go back to school, and I couldn't see myself doing anything with the degree. After a few months of wrestling with The Lord, I finally agreed. I didn't even ask the Lord what university He wanted me to attend; I just reluctantly signed up at the local university I attended for my bachelor's degree. I took the summer class, and the entire time, I felt like it just wasn't relevant. I was teaching in a private Christian school, and the teachings of this secular university didn't match up with what we were doing at my school.

After finishing one class, I told my husband I had been obedient to what I felt God was calling me to do, but I just didn't have a complete peace about it. When the fall semester came, I did not re-enroll. Then spring semester came, and I still didn't have peace. Feeling frustrated, I cried out to the Lord for two weeks, asking Him to reveal Himself in a clear way. I had to come to the place in my relationship with Him I wanted to do what He called me to, but I wanted to do it wholeheartedly. I needed an attitude adjustment, so I asked the Lord to change my heart to match His heart. I knew He had the perfect plan for me even if it didn't match mine. I had walked with the Lord long enough to see His faithfulness, and I did trust Him.

In the second week of praying specifically, I got a "random" email from California Baptist University that literally said, "Are you interested in an Educational Leadership Master's for Faith-Based schools?" I had never heard of such a degree and I was skeptical. Was there really a master's degree for faith-based schools?

I feel a little foolish as I type this testimony because it is so clear now this was God hand delivering an invitation to what I had been asking Him to reveal. But overthinking it all, I didn't respond. It seemed so random because I had no connection to this university. How did they get my email, and why did they choose me? Two days later they sent me another email, this time, a personal one from the director. How much clearer could the Lord make it?

Thankfully, the Lord knows how stubborn I am, and He kept pursuing me. I spoke to the director and immediately felt complete peace. Without a doubt, I knew this was where He was calling me.

As I continued to speak with the director over several weeks, he told me the degree was all online, except for two weeks in the summer when I would be on campus taking the first classes. Seriously? I live in Louisiana, and this college is in California. When I heard that, I immediately felt disappointed because I knew I couldn't leave my family for two weeks. The doubt crept in.

As I struggled with this doubt, I cried out to God, asking Him to go before me. As I pressed into Him, I could hear the soft whispers of "Wait." During the next week, God continued to work in the waiting. A friend was over for dinner one night, and we were catching up. I told her what God was calling me to, and I told her my reservation about leaving my family for two weeks. I learned her in-laws live in Riverside,

California, seven miles from the university I would attend! They were planning a visit that very summer, and she offered to come with me and watch my kids while I was at school.

Now I understand the "waiting." I sat in tears, realizing just how intricately detailed our God orchestrates everything! Who would have ever thought this "random" email was really God, hand delivering the invitation for me to follow His will!?

As I worked through the degree, I came to love everything the Lord was teaching me. And then came the time for the dreaded research class. Knowing I had taken it that summer at my local university, I wasn't looking forward to it. This semester, in which the research class was to be taken, was a hard one for me as my parents were going through a divorce after 30 years of marriage. I struggled daily to make it through the days ahead of me, wondering where God was in it. But He showed up mightily when I discovered my research class from my local university would count, and I did not have to take it again!

This meant I had that semester off, and I could work through the personal things so heavy on my heart with my parents' divorce.

If I am being honest, I saw attending my local university as a mistake that cost me time and money that summer. But the Lord knew the hard days coming in my personal life and used that very "mistake" to allow me to be off school the very semester I needed. If we humble ourselves before Him and seek Him, He will waste nothing.

Romans 8:28 says, "And we know that in all things God works for the good of those who love Him and have been called according to His purpose." I love how He shows up in personal ways to show us just how true and relevant His word is to us.

The best part about this story is that I currently use that degree as I am now the principal at the Christian school that I've been a part of for almost a decade. While I never had a desire or even thought about being a principal, He once again changed my heart to match His, and I could imagine doing nothing else. I wake up feeling fulfilled knowing I am exactly where He wants me. And it all started with a simple yes, several years ago!

DEVOTION
andrea bourgeois

I have heard this popular Proverb 3:5-6 for years and after hearing it so often, I almost dismiss the power it holds now because it seems cliché. Truthfully and sadly, it's almost like my brain has heard it so often that it seems it's lost its power. But that just isn't true.

While trying to figure out how and what we will do with our home because of the damage from the storm, the Lord spoke this verse, CLEARLY. It's not that "overused" verse any longer. It's real. Nothing about this storm and its aftermath makes sense. Nothing about our situation makes sense, but God is revealing His power and His plans little by little. It's an everlasting mystery being unfolded one layer at a time. And I have only to trust and acknowledge Him and He'll make my path straight!

God is notorious for guiding us through the unknown that makes little sense! The world tells us things are impossible, but does the world know our God?

As storms come, they might change us, and our futures might not make sense now… but God's got us in His hands! He's never failed us! He makes a way!

God may tell you to stay with your spouse after an affair, and yet the world will think you're crazy. God may tell you to quit your well-paying job to start a business, and your family and friends will try to talk you out of it. God may tell you to go back to school, yet it will make no sense to you. God could open doors and opportunities for you for a home that was an unreachable dream for so long.

He makes a way when there is no way! God is in the business of getting us to do things that make little sense because He sees the bigger picture.

"TRUST IN THE LORD WITH ALL YOUR HEART
AND LEAN NOT ON YOUR OWN UNDERSTANDING;
IN ALL YOUR WAYS ACKNOWLEDGE HIM AND HE
WILL MAKE YOUR PATHS STRAIGHT."

Proverbs 3:5-6

SURVIVAL KIT FOR THE STORM

samantha larocque
Licensed Clinical Social Worker

Despair can come in many shapes and forms. Despair can leave us with undeniable pain and paralyze us. I've dealt with despair in my own life, I see it daily in my private practice, in my family, friends, and of course, in social media outlets. It's something none of us are immune to. Each individual handles it differently, with so many of us handling it in silence.

Satan wants nothing more than for us to feel isolated, shamed, and rejected. He likes to accuse us and confuse us with what we think, feel, and how we react. My heart's desire is to see the value we place on our overall mental health improve, as we understand THE CREATOR created us. Whether the impact Coronavirus has had on us all has been your first traumatic event, or you are someone with battle scars from life, there is hope. Whether you have dealt with mental health issues or are experiencing crippling anxiety for the first time, there is hope. If you have been able to pick up the pieces to find normalcy again, or if you are feeling more hopeless than before, there is hope.

Two truths that we know from scripture are that we are CREATED for a purpose and that we have a mighty protector.

God addressed those issues by breathing scriptures into life, before you even needed those promises. When we remain in silence about the issues we are dealing with/the pain we are feeling, Satan victories in our isolation. When we do something to deliberately hurt our bodies or sabotage what His purpose for our life is, Satan victories in our shame. When we walk away from the community because of the shame we feel, Satan wins in our feelings of rejection.

There may be things you are struggling with from childhood, early adulthood, the present, or the uncertainty of the future. Maybe you are having individual issues, maybe they are within your family. Every person reacts to stress differently, but the one thing we have in common is that we all REACT. There is nothing wrong with you, it's biological!

Comparison is the thief of joy, so be careful to compare yourself to others and think "I'm the only one with this problem".

A diagnosis of Major Depression Disorder, Anxiety, Mood Disorder, Post Traumatic Stress Disorder, or a family history of these issues prior to a stressor will affect the way you are triggered.

The depth of our reaction is based on our brain development. We've all heard of the "fight or flight" response, which begins in the brain. Our brain perceives a threat, our brain alerts our body, our body reacts with a physical and emotional symptom. It is also intertwined with hormones that are released to allow our body to react. That hormone is called Cortisol. It gives our body the adrenaline needed to get through the threat we are facing. If you are someone with a childhood life experience of trauma, abuse, and/or neglect, your brain development has been affected by this. Sometimes, an adult survivor of these things can be more reactive to stressors. When dealing with stress, anxiety, or trauma, it is also common for our emotions to "take over" our rational thoughts.

This can cause a decrease in memory function (fog), a decrease in emotion regulation (meltdown/irritability), and an increase in hyperactivity and fear response (jumpy/flash backs, insomnia). Long term exposure to these things could lead to a medical or mental health crisis.

To handle these stressors effectively and manage these symptoms, coping skills are put into place. Coping skills can be positive or negative.

Negative coping skills are developed when we are looking for immediate gratification and healing. Unfortunately, there is no magic wand to heal from trauma.

Positive coping skills take time to work effectively and often take practice in incorporating them.

Coping skills become your "tool box" or "tool belt" with easily accessible tools to help you complete the task at hand.

Remember these take time and practice to notice positive changes in your reactions.

You may need to examine whether professional help during these difficult times would be beneficial to you, for an objective view.

This is not a sign of weakness. God called very qualified people into this profession for a purpose. The door is there, you just have to knock.

Romans 8:31 states, "If God is for us, who can be against us."

I PRAY THAT YOU HAVE BEEN AFFIRMED IN
WHO YOU ARE
AND KNOW THAT
YOU ARE NOT ALONE
IN YOUR TRIALS AND TRIBULATIONS.

IT IS OKAY TO NOT BE OKAY, BUT DON'T STAY THERE!

YOUR COPING SKILLS
TOOLBOX

Coping skills to help with anxiety/stress may include:

DEEP BREATHING

LISTENING TO MUSIC

READING YOUR BIBLE

PRAYER

MEMORIZING SCRIPTURE

PLACING SCRIPTURE AROUND YOUR HOUSE

EXAMINING YOUR BOUNDARIES TO ASSESS
IF YOU ARE BEING STRETCHED TOO THIN

MAKING BETTER CHOICES WHEN
IT COMES TO NUTRITION

GETTING THE PROPER SLEEP

INCORPORATING PHYSICAL ACTIVITY
INTO YOUR DAY/WEEK

POSITIVE AFFIRMATIONS

REACHING OUT TO A FRIEND

ATTENDING A CHURCH SERVICE

FINDING A SUPPORT SYSTEM

PURPOSE

andrea bourgeois

A few days after Laura, when we were home, we could get spotty cell service to contact friends and family to hear how their homes did in the storm. Many people were posting pictures of the damages to Facebook to show their extended family and friends in other parts of the country what Laura did. My heart was shattered as I saw a co-worker and friend's picture of the remains of their home with her and her husband standing in it with their American Flag flying high behind them. They have a little girl our son's age, and all I could think about was what she and her kids must be feeling as they see all their belongings scattered in shreds across their yard. The following post was about a friend who lives in another part of our country, carrying on with life as usual. Her life hadn't come to a screeching halt like ours. She was joyful and excited about her kids starting school. I saw lots of posts like that, and it stung a little that they did not know what we were facing down here. The weather channel and mainstream media quickly stopped all coverage of the destruction and aftermath. After all, in their opinion, our state fared much better than expected because we didn't have the twenty-foot storm surge they had predicted. When in all actuality, this was the worst storm to hit the gulf coast in over 150 years, and the damage was catastrophic. After Rita in '05, we had damage, but not near as bad as this. Businesses were back and running within days, and the homes destroyed were a fraction of what Laura did to us. So bitterness raged within me as the media was more worried about wearing masks and what other political charades they needed to blast instead of our hurting city.

My city was grieving while the world was rejoicing in the small things within our quarantine limitations. It was no one's fault per se. It just didn't feel fair. It brought me back to when I was going through my divorce. I attended five weddings that spring while my life was slipping through my fingertips. All my friends were happy and getting married, and my marriage was falling apart. Or when we were trying to get pregnant, baby bumps greeted me everywhere! I attended multiple baby showers and birthday parties that took every bit of strength I had in me not to burst into tears while I was there.

Life does this to us. While we are hurting, others not affected carry on. We accept that and not take it personally. As much as we want the world to stop with us, it doesn't. About the same time, we were in the middle of survival with weeks of no power, I saw California and Oregon's fires. I wondered, had we not been dealing with Laura, would I be sensitive to others and their struggles on the other side of our country?

I prayed for those affected by the fires and was way more intentional than I probably would have been. We can't empathize until we've lived it. When I hear of someone struggling through a divorce or infertility, my heart genuinely hurts for them, and I can pray and be there for them in ways only because I've been there. The same goes for natural disasters. Now, I get it. I can genuinely walk along with someone who's in the storm with empathy, just not sympathy.

Look back on your life's storms. How did God heal, restore, or mend your brokenness? Your past pain is someone else's new journey. Comfort those God puts in your path because He comforted you.

FIND GOD'S PURPOSE IN YOUR PAIN!
AND THEN ... YOUR PURPOSE IS TO TELL YOUR STORY -
SO TELL IT WELL.

"I TELL YOU THE TRUTH; YOU WILL WEEP AND MOURN
WHILE THE WORLD REJOICES. YOU WILL GRIEVE, BUT
YOUR GRIEF WILL TURN TO JOY. A WOMAN GIVING BIRTH
TO A CHILD HAS PAIN BECAUSE HER TIME HAS COME, BUT
WHEN HER BABY IS BORN, SHE FORGETS THE ANGUISH
BECAUSE OF HER JOY THAT A CHILD IS BORN INTO THE
WORLD. SO WITH YOU: NOW IS YOUR TIME OF GRIEF, BUT
I WILL SEE YOU AGAIN, AND YOU WILL REJOICE, AND NO
ONE WILL TAKE AWAY YOUR JOY."

John 16: 20-22

"PRAISE BE TO THE GOD AND FATHER OF OUR LORD
JESUS CHRIST, THE FATHER OF COMPASSION AND THE
GOD OF ALL COMFORT, WHO COMFORTS US IN ALL OUR
TROUBLES SO THAT WE CAN COMFORT THOSE IN ANY
TROUBLE WITH THE COMFORT WE RECEIVE FROM GOD.
FOR JUST AS WE SHARE ABUNDANTLY IN THE SUFFERINGS
OF CHRIST, SO ALSO OUR COMFORT ABOUNDS THROUGH
CHRIST. IF WE ARE DISTRESSED, IT IS FOR YOUR COMFORT
AND SALVATION; IF WE ARE COMFORTED, IT IS FOR
YOUR COMFORT, WHICH PRODUCES IN YOU PATIENT
ENDURANCE OF THE SAME SUFFERINGS WE SUFFER. AND
OUR HOPE FOR YOU IS FIRM BECAUSE WE KNOW THAT
JUST AS YOU SHARE IN OUR SUFFERINGS, SO ALSO YOU
SHARE IN OUR COMFORT."

2 Corinthians 1:3-7

ALSO BY ANDREA P. BOURGEOIS

JUST
BREATHE
A Modern-Day Exodus Journey
to Revive Your
SOUL

Andrea P.
BOURGEOIS